ENOUGH IS ENOUGH

All proceeds from this publication will be donated to *The February 14th Fund for the Forward, Together Forward Scholars* at Northern Illinois University and the *Hokie Spirit Memorial Fund* at Virginia Polytechnic Institute and State University.

Enough is Enough

a student affairs perspective on preparedness
and response to a campus shooting

Edited by
Brian O. Hemphill and
Brandi Hephner LaBanc

Foreword by
Gwendolyn Jordan Dungy and Gregory Roberts

A JOINT PUBLICATION OF

STERLING, VIRGINIA

COPYRIGHT © 2010 BY ACPA, COLLEGE
STUDENT EDUCATORS INTERNATIONAL, AND
NASPA, THE NATIONAL ASSOCIATION OF
STUDENT PERSONNEL ADMINISTRATORS, INC.

Published by Stylus Publishing, LLC
22883 Quicksilver Drive
Sterling, Virginia 20166–2102

Cover design by Yuma Nakada

Library of Congress Cataloging-in-Publication-Data
Hemphill, Brian O.
   Enough is enough : a student affairs perspective on
preparedness and response to a campus shooting / edited
by Brian O. Hemphill and Brandi Hephner LaBanc ;
foreword by Gwendolyn Jordan Dungy and Gregory
Roberts.—1st ed.
       p.   cm.
   Includes bibliographical references.
   ISBN 978-1-57922-442-4 (cloth : alk. paper)
   ISBN 978-1-57922-443-1 (pbk. : alk. paper)
1. Campus violence—United States.   2. Campus
violence—United States—Prevention.   3. School
shootings—United States.   4. School shootings—United
States—Prevention.   5. Student affairs services—United
States.   6. Universities and colleges—United States—
Safety measures.   I. LaBanc, Brandi Hephner.   II. Title.
LB2345.H46   2010
378.1'9782—dc22
                                              2010004316

13-digit ISBN: 978-1-57922-442-4 (cloth)
13-digit ISBN: 978-1-57922-443-1(paper)

Printed in the United States of America

All first editions printed on acid free paper
that meets the American National Standards Institute

Z39-48 Standard.

> Bulk Purchases
>
> Quantity discounts are available for use in workshops
> and for staff development.
> Call 1-800-232-0223

First Edition, 2010

10   9   8   7   6   5   4   3   2   1

Dedicated to Zenobia Lawrence Hikes
(August 27, 1955–October 27, 2008)

In March 2008 our good friend and esteemed colleague Zenobia Lawrence Hikes gave the closing keynote address at the National Association of Student Personnel Administrators (NASPA) Annual Conference. Having represented the administration of Virginia Tech with calm and eloquence through months of media attention following the unprecedented April 16, 2007, shootings on her campus, Hikes shared with her colleagues in student affairs what had happened and what had been learned through the tragedy. She reminded us that no one is immune to terror and that we must all prepare for the unimaginable. Declaring, "Enough is enough," she called upon us to act with a "fierce urgency" to stem the tide of societal violence before new students arrive at our nation's campuses. The conference participants appeared to have experienced something of a catharsis as a result of her speech, spontaneously rising to their feet—through tears—for a long standing ovation.

Just prior to this conference our campus was the site of another shooting. The support and advice Hikes was willing and able to offer were invaluable as we responded to the unthinkable and began to facilitate the healing process for our campus community. Indeed, upon her untimely passing, student affairs administrators from across the country attested to how her willingness to share lessons learned from Virginia Tech had made their campuses safer. In fact, what she described went far beyond lessons learned—those who heard her speak at the NASPA conference talked for months about how she touched their hearts and inspired them.

The American College Personnel Association (ACPA) governing board and its entire membership approved and presented a resolution in honor of Hikes in March 2009. Her two sisters were present to receive this most sincere acknowledgment of Hikes's contributions to the profession and ACPA's appreciation for all Zenobia had done for American higher education. They told the audience how "wonderful [it was] to know that her colleagues and peers across the country respected her work."

A year after Hikes's moving speech at the NASPA conference, the spontaneous, long, and tearful standing ovation was repeated as Amber Hikes accepted NASPA's Scott Goodnight Award for Outstanding Service as a senior student affairs administrator on her mother's behalf. In so doing, she reminded those assembled that her mother had "charged a nation, a community, a world of student affairs leaders by asserting 'Enough is enough.'"

The Enough is Enough campaign (see http//www.Enoughis Enoughcampaign.org) initiated by NASPA past president Diana Doyle in response to Hikes's call to action is in many ways Zenobia's legacy, yet it is much more than one person's vision. We must all take up the charge Hikes gave us and commit to collaborating and doing all within our power to stem the tide of violence in the very place students *should* feel safest—within the academy. This book is just one contribution to that effort; those who have experienced campus tragedy share their experiences for the benefit of others just as Zenobia so willingly did. While this book is lovingly and fittingly dedicated to Hikes's memory, as this subject matter became a passion for her, we would be remiss if our memory of the courageous woman who was Zenobia Lawrence Hikes was limited to her response to the Virginia Tech tragedy. As her daughter reminded us at the NASPA awards luncheon, Zenobia "was a powerful woman who survived incredible life events—among them, April 16, 2007."

Contents

Acknowledgments

WE ARE ESPECIALLY THANKFUL and forever indebted for the support provided by Clare Andres and Mary Spring who were there with us through the darkest hours of the tragedy, and certainly helped us make this project a reality.

Likewise, we are grateful and honored to have the support of our leadership at Northern Illinois University. We extend a special thank-you to president John G. Peters, executive vice president and provost Raymond W. Alden III, and executive vice president and chief of operations Eddie R. Williams.

We also appreciate the support and guidance of our professional associations. Through the endorsement and encouragement provided by Gwen Dungy, Greg Roberts, and Kaaryn Sanon, we were able to bring our story and lessons learned to others in the field.

BRIAN O. HEMPHILL
Northern Illinois University

BRANDI HEPHNER LaBANC
Northern Illinois University

Foreword

IN THE WAKE OF April 16, 2007, and what would be called the worst
school shooting in U.S. history, Zenobia Lawrence Hikes, vice president for student affairs, represented the administration and students
of Virginia Tech with the highest level of professionalism. With calm
demeanor and eloquence she was a responsive and collaborative
campus leader through the months of media and law enforcement
attention. Within a year of the tragic shootings on her campus, Hikes
graciously agreed to be a keynote speaker at the 2008 National Association of Student Personnel Administrators (NASPA) Annual Conference, sharing lessons learned to guide her professional colleagues
if they someday should need to respond to severe campus violence.

Just weeks before the March conference, Hikes's expertise—
earned in an area none willingly seeks—was brought to bear working
with Brian O. Hemphill, vice president for student affairs and enrollment management at Northern Illinois University, when he found his
campus in similar circumstances following the February 14, 2008,
campus shootings at that institution.

The germination of the idea for this book and the value it could
represent to their colleagues came from subsequent conversations
between Hikes and Hemphill about their shared experience of active
shooter situations and all that the aftermath of those crises entailed
in their roles as leaders on campus. Beyond their personal and professional reflections through speeches and contact with the media, they
wanted to contribute significantly in a more permanent manner to
higher education. This book represents that contribution to the
improvement and professionalization of our practice.

While NASPA, the American College Personnel Association
(ACPA), and countless other associations representing student affairs
and beyond have been working to address devastating occurrences of

campus violence, nothing is so powerful nor so instructive as the firsthand accounts in this book written by professionals who have lived through the crisis, continue to heal while facilitating the healing of their campus community, and offer true on-the-ground counsel for their colleagues (see chapter 9) who hopefully will never have to put into practice its full scope.

No one pursues a profession in student affairs for times such as these, but "the care and support of the campus community displayed in the aftermath of a tragedy reveals the strength, resolve, and true character of an institution" (see chapter 6, p. 115), and the *character* of an institution rests in the individuals who make up the campus community, from students to faculty, staff, and administrators; to alumni; and all those who touch the community. Truly in times of crisis, the walls of what separate us come tumbling down, as we recognize that not only is every facet of a campus community touched but that campuses are not ivory towers. Rather, they are living, breathing organisms intimately connected with the world (see chapter 7). Indeed, in today's connected world, a campus tragedy is felt not only by the surrounding community but by campuses and communities across the state, the nation, and even the world.

What seems particularly tragic about campus shootings is that they shatter the myth of the academy as a kind of safe haven. While statistics show that campuses are indeed safer than the real world in terms of murder rates, this is little comfort when the functional and familial ideals of the academy are threatened, as described in chapter 1.

"Deeply entrenched values at the core of the academic enterprise shape how institutions conduct their affairs," writes Raymond W. Alden III, from a provost's perspective (see p. 137 in chapter 7). Some of the values identified are the discovery of knowledge, individual and institutional autonomy, freedom of inquiry and expression, commitment to shared decision making, and striking a balance between "sometimes competing interests of the individual and the common good" (p. 137). When campus violence erupts, all these values are called into question and tested in the institution's response to the crisis. Just as the nation had to face difficult questions in the wake of 9/11, when matters of security and fundamental civil liberties seemed at odds, so too do campuses face competing demands in emergency management.

Further complicating matters are the federal requirements around emergency management and reporting, as further codified in the Higher Education Opportunity Act of 2008 and various state laws that administrators must always be cognizant of and balance in their work. Those in student affairs and others across campus are left with the daunting task of planning for the unknown and trying to manage the unmanageable. Chapter 3 offers invaluable guidance on all-hazards planning and the level of detail that demands ongoing attention. As the authors of this chapter indicate on p. 58, there is a "distinct difference between simply having a solid conceptual model or plan for crisis response and having an active CRT [crisis response team]." While we can never prepare for *everything*, we *can* develop an all-campus-personnel crisis response as a learned behavior.

As with any traumatic event, the effects of a campus shooting are wide ranging and must be approached with a long-term perspective. The authors of chapter 4 offer insight related to typical reactions during times of crisis and offer guidance for counseling from the immediate aftermath—more "psychological first aid" (see p. 84) than traditional counseling—to the months and years following a campus shooting. While the needs of student survivors and victims' families are always paramount, it is essential that faculty and staff heed *self-care* if they are to be effective in their care for others' needs.

At some point, there is inevitably a yearning for things to return to normal, but this can only be achieved through struggle and the ultimate recognition that there can only be a *new normal*. The authors of chapter 6 offer further advice on healing the campus community, stating that the opportunities the institution provides for people to heal following a tragedy "are the foundation for an institution to lead its community to a new normal" (p. 131). Recognizing that each community is unique, there are no best practices but only effective strategies to be used and adapted to fit the community as deemed most appropriate.

In considering the long-term needs of the campus, the authors of chapter 2 explore the connection between emotional health and violence, offering thoughts on prevention, intervention, and resiliency. While a comparison of campus shooters provides no single profile, two general commonalities emerge. First, by and large, the shooters are men, suggesting there is work to be done regarding a social construction of masculinity that accepts anger and aggression as normal and conversely impedes seeking help. Second, the latest and most egregious shootings, in high schools and institutions of postsecondary education alike, have been homicide-suicides, in which the ultimate aim seems to have been more about what the shooter saw as a "glorious" way of ending his own unsatisfactory life. More students with a mental health diagnosis are entering college today than ever before, and in the vast majority of cases they will have a successful educational career and never be a threat to anyone. There remains, though, a great demand for resources and training sufficient to appropriately meet the mental health needs of all our students and to ensure they have all the tools at their disposal to achieve success in the academic environment.

Strong essential services are imperative with the growing concerns of campus violence across the country (see chapter 5), and student affairs professionals are often called upon to manage these critical functions. As educators, practitioners, and administrators, student affairs professionals are uniquely situated to address not only the physical safety and well-being of community members but also their mental health. Throughout crisis management, we should not neglect our roles as resource builders, educators, listeners, and healers.

Although we may never know *why* such violence occurs, we must heed the call to collaborate and use resources such as this volume to help us determine *what* to do to stem the tide of violence before and when it reaches college and university campuses while understanding that regardless of all we do to attempt to prevent and intervene, we will not always be successful. While hindsight seems to prove the notion that "it won't happen on my campus" is naive, in many ways keeping this notion is the only way we can live and function day to day while simultaneously planning and preparing for something we cannot possibly imagine. As the authors write in chapter 1, safety ultimately rests in "neither underreacting nor overreacting" (p. 33).

NASPA and ACPA stand ready to help further the collaborations and professional development of skills suggested in this book. As professional associations, we are charged with constructing and disseminating knowledge. These authors have the knowledge that practitioners are seeking and will use. We welcome this contribution to the field of knowledge and to assisting educators, practitioners, and administrators in improving our professional practice. The changing nature of the world we live in demands that professionals seek a new way to address crises. That is why this book is so timely and timeless; we can learn from those who have gone before us and do all in our power to prevent the same situations from being repeated. We must continue to work to build stronger, more responsive, caring campus communities so that such incidents can be averted when possible and responded to effectively when they cannot. The value of this book is the underlying current that reminds us that our campus communities are resilient and do recover. While violence is senseless, tragic, and claims innocent victims, it does not ultimately prevail. We are reminded through the voices contained here why we *did* choose a career in student affairs—for the lives we touch, the communities we are a part of, and the honor of playing whatever small role we are assigned in the growth and development of the students we are privileged to work with.

GWENDOLYN JORDAN DUNGY
NASPA Executive Director

GREGORY ROBERTS
ACPA Executive Director

1 Violence in the Shadow of the Ivory Tower

Murder at the University

Richard J. Ferraro and Blanche McHugh

IN THE American imagination, the ideal university (henceforth understood to include universities and colleges) is an institution of social harmony built on charitable foundations that works to enhance the intellectual abilities and professional capabilities of all members of a collaborative academic community. A prerequisite for the fulfillment of this ideal is relative nonviolence: The university must offer a modicum of good order, social stability, and reasoned behavior if it is to deal effectively with teaching, research, and service delivered by a diverse population in a plethora of fields and courses of study.

The University as a Safe Haven

This functional ideal is lent support by a familial ideal. When parents send their sons and daughters to a university, they imagine the destination is a safe haven. They expect their offspring will have a positive and mostly pleasant experience at the minimum, or at the maximum even fundamentally transform themselves personally and professionally after 4 years. Further, they anticipate that occasional stresses and setbacks will be offset by general happiness and broad accomplishments. This is why many parents say they *entrust* their sons and daughters to a university, even though there are no real legal or contractual bases for defining students as objects accepted in trust.

These functional and familial ideals can be intruded upon by social offenses (such as abuse of alcohol), economic challenges (e.g., significant cuts in external support or overreliance on consumerist models), biased expression (e.g., epithets or stereotyping), and so on. However, the university is most challenged when it comes to murder, literally, for murder potentially transforms the university from a nursery for hope and promising young leaders into a graveyard of despair and lost youth, for people affected directly and for those touched by it.

For many, a university is much safer than the real world. Campus murder rates are indeed lower than they are in the general population (Centers for Disease Control and Prevention, 2008). However, this accurate comparative point is of small comfort when it comes to functional and familial ideals, since expectations for the university are much higher than those that apply to other institutions such as a town, workplace, or corporation. The university, for better or worse, is expected to be—and needs to be—an institution especially committed to life and safety.

Single and Double Murders: Clery and Beyond Clery

It is not easy to obtain an accurate count of all members of the university (students, faculty, and staff) who have been the object of murder. To get a rough preliminary indication, one logically begins by reviewing statistics from the Jean Clery Disclosure of Campus Security Policy and Campus Crime Statistics Act (1992; henceforth referred to as the Clery Act) that track criminal activity including homicide on campuses and in the immediate bordering areas (Security on Campus, 2009).

A global overview of pertinent murder statistics can be obtained by using summary findings reported by the U.S. Department of Education (2007) for the years 2005–2007, a 3-year period of systematic collection, aggregation, and gross reporting of data in keeping with the ongoing development of Clery Act regulations and practices. (Such systematic data collection, aggregation, and reporting is not available for years prior to 2005; statistics for 2008 were not available when this book went to press.)

For 2005, 28 murder victims were reported for the several thousand postsecondary institutions that provided information under the Clery Act (including public and private, profit and nonprofit, religious and secular, 2-year and 4-year, graduate and undergraduate, professional and nonprofessional colleges and universities). For 2006, for the same group of schools, the number declined to 25 victims; for 2007 the number jumped to 64, but that large increase is mostly explained by 32 murders in April of that year at Virginia Polytechnic Institute and State University (Virginia Tech). From these data, it is reasonable to assert that a fraction of 1% of postsecondary schools in the United States experienced a murder in any 1 of the 3 years in question (U.S. Department of Education, 2007).

One might wonder if that *relatively* small percentage for homicide is made still more compact by the inclusion of 2-year schools and proprietary 4-year institutions. It could be argued that such schools—which on average may have a smaller residential presence, more compact physical plants, shorter hours of attendance on campus, and more nontraditional students—may also have significantly fewer risk factors for homicide in Clery Act terms, and thus may disproportionately reduce the overall average. To test that possibility, the U.S. Department of Education (2007) compiled a list of 1,387 four-year nonprofit colleges and universities. It included large and small, public and private institutions, drawn from all 50 states. For the years 2005, 2006, and 2007, complete entries were obtained for all 1,387 schools (see Table 1.1).

Clery Act data for this broad sample of 4-year, nonprofit schools, still indicate a *relatively* safe picture. For any year in this 3-year

Table 1.1   Homicides on Campus, 2005, 2006, 2007

Year	Number of Schools	Number of Schools With at Least One Murder	Percent of Schools in Sample With at Least One Murder	Number of People Killed in Assembled Sample
2007	1,387	19	1.37	51
2006	1,387	14	1.01	16
2005	1,387	10	.072	10

period, 98% to 99% of universities and colleges reported no homicides. There is an increase over an admittedly narrow 3-year time span, as the number of affected schools rises slightly from .072% to 1.37%, and the jump from 10 to 16 to 51 dead from 2005 to 2007 seems quite alarming. However, as noted previously, much of that increase in 2007 is accounted for by one extraordinary incident, that is, the mass slayings at Virginia Tech in April. In the vast majority of cases where homicide occurred over this 3-year period, one or two people were killed per incident.

Moving farther back to the years 2000 through 2004 for this same sample of 1,387 colleges and universities, more fragmentary data were reported (see Table 1.2).

The difference between Table 1.1 (1,387 entries) and Table 1.2 (405–536 entries), and specifically the slight increase in the frequency of schools affected by murder, can likely be accounted for by the fact that Table 1.2 includes proportionally fewer small schools. Still, on this narrower sample, the range of 1.6% to 2.35% means that about 97% to 98% of universities and colleges would be spared even a single reported homicide on campus or in the immediately adjacent area in any particular year of this 5-year period.

However, Clery Act statistics do draw a narrow circumference, touching only the campus and immediately adjacent property. In truth, when it comes to the safety of university faculty, staff, and especially students, there really are three pertinent geographical loci: (a) the campus with its buildings, grounds, and immediately adjacent environs; (b) the larger hinterland, consisting of the greater

Table 1.2   Homicides on Campus, 2000–2004

Year	Number of Schools	Number of Schools With at Least One Murder	Percent of Schools in Sample With at Least One Murder	Number of People Killed in Assembled Sample
2004	425	10	2.35	17
2003	536	8	1.87	9
2002	476	8	1.68	15
2001	437	7	1.60	9
2000	405	7	1.73	9

neighborhood and nearby town, city, or county; and (c) more remote locations, such as a distant family home, an external internship or cooperative site, study abroad, and so on. Obviously, the university's greatest legal and ethical responsibility pertains to campus, but when a student (or faculty or staff member) is murdered in any one of the three loci, it affects that individual, his or her kith and kin, and diminishes the entire university community to some extent.

In addition, it is important to obtain not only some basic numbers on the frequency of murder but also salient facts that relate to the cases (where they occurred, what was the cause, what sorts of weapon were used, etc.), so campus administrators can make minimal sense of what occurred and try to take preventive action.

To get a basic, broad picture of murders of university students, faculty, and staff, comprehensive Internet checking was completed by the authors; 262 cases were collected in which the subject was murder of people affiliated with a university (mostly students but also occasionally faculty and staff) between the years 2000 and 2008. (Information was collected on more than 100 additional cases from 1965 to 1999, but those cases likely represent a very small number of the applicable universe, especially with respect to the 1960s and 1970s.) It cannot be claimed that the 262 cases considered for the first 8 years of this decade represent a true scientific survey. It is likely that the Internet, reflecting a broad range of journalistic practices, would tend to pick up disproportionately the more interesting or dramatic of cases, nor can one pretend to have assembled even a majority of relevant cases for 2000–2008. Further, the likelihood that the Internet tends to employ popular rather than scholarly sources should be acknowledged, possibly entailing an increase in inaccuracy of detail. However, the assembled data for the present decade offer a broad-based view of the matter at hand.

Researchers made certain exclusions in collecting cases: (a) negligent homicides (e.g., driving under the influence [DUI] or unintentional alcohol poisoning), (b) deaths involving late-term or just-born babies (this seemed to belong to the topic of abortion), (c) speculative cases where it was not clear that murder took place (e.g., the so-called Smiley Face Murders where accidentally drowned students might have been mislabeled as murder victims), (d) and missing persons cases (those likely rooted in flight rather than foul play; Piehl, 2008).

Table 1.3 tabulates the 262 cases by the number of people murdered per incident at the university. Out of respect for innocents here and throughout this chapter, people who kill themselves after murdering others are not counted as murder victims. They are instead considered "special-circumstance" suicides. Also excluded for present purposes are nonfatal casualties, meaning those who were wounded or injured.

It is clear that when homicide occurs in relation to university people—at least according to this sample—in the vast majority of instances, it involves a single victim.

The causes for single murders occasionally relate to mental health issues. For example, in May 2003, Biswanath Halder, a 62-year-old former student, who suffered from depression and delusions of persecution and who had trouble maintaining minimal self-care, conducted a 7-hour gun battle with police on the campus of Case Western Reserve University in which miraculously only one person was killed (Kropko, 2005). Sometimes a single murder is rooted in discrimination (such as with Jesse Valencia, of the University of Missouri, who was killed in 2004 by Steven Rios to cover up a gay relationship; Slavit, 2008). Sexual predators whose given names or nicknames have become infamous, like Ted Bundy, the Hillside Strangler, and the Rainy Day Murderer, alongside less-notorious sexual offenders, were frequently found (Larsen, 1980; Nelson, 1994;

Table 1.3   Murders of University People: 2000–2008

Number of People Killed	Number of Incidents
Single person	234
2 people	22
3 people	4
4 people	0
5 people	1
6 people	0
7 people	0
> 7 people	1

Table 1.4   Locations of Murders

Location	Number of Cases
On campus	37
Off campus	183
Remote location	29
Total known cases	**249**

Rainy Day Murders, 1969; Schwarz, 2004). However, other common reasons are rooted in robbery, burglary, carjacking, professional or personal jealousy, escalating verbal and physical altercations, gang activity, drug dealing, and/or domestic violence.

The causes that pertain to single murders also tend to apply to double murders. One murder escalates to two generally because of situational factors. For example, two people rather than one walking home at night might create the occasion for a double rather than a single murder if a mugging takes place, or the obsessed individual who confronts an ex-partner might fatally harm another if the intended victim is in the company of a friend or associate when contact occurs.

Table 1.4 records where murderous events took place in which one or two people were killed (a sample of 249 cases).

The results indicate that campuses, given their community focus, self-containment (in many cases), and extended protection (oversight ranging from resident assistants to campus police) tend to be less dangerous than off-campus locations. In addition, while the line allotted to remote locations has the lowest single entry, considering the number of students and the amount of time spent on campus as opposed to the same measures for remote locations, the advantage in protection falls to the former category rather than the latter.

In single and double murders, Table 1.5 records the principal means of administering death.

Guns, especially handguns, are by far the most common single means death is administered in cases involving one or two fatalities on campus (in this sample); however, knives are not insignificant in the picture. Further, strangulation is relatively common, especially in cases associated with sexual assault.

Table 1.5   Principal Means of Administering Death

Death Delivered By	Number of Cases
Gun	99
Knife or other cutting instrument	61
Strangulation or suffocation	34
Beating (fists or object)	28
Other (car, drugs, fire, etc.)	8
Total number of cases with known means	**230**

It also should be asked if the source of the violence is internal or external. For example, in September and October of 2000, two 19-year-old Gallaudet University students, were killed on campus in separate incidents by blunt force trauma in one case and stabbing in the other. The killer was Joseph Mesa, another Gallaudet student (Ramsland, 2004). However, in January 2007, a University of Tennessee alumnus and his student girlfriend were abducted from an off-campus restaurant and tortured, raped, and killed by a group of men (and one woman) not associated with any university (Sanchez, 2007). The University of Tennessee incident was graphically much more violent and disturbing, but the Gallaudet incident was haunting in a different way because the enemy came from within.

Table 1.6 shows known entries for the sample collected between 2000 and 2008.

It is clear that a majority of murders that involve students, faculty, and staff cannot be attributed to people who study or work at the

Table 1.6   University Murder Victims: Affiliation or Nonaffiliation With the University

Affiliation of Victim and Murderer	Number of Cases
Victim and murderer affiliated with same university	46
Victim and murderer affiliated with different universities	10
Victim is a university member/killer is not	134
Killer is a university member/victim is not	14
Total known cases	**204**

same university; however, the number of cases in which members of the community do turn on each other (46 out of 204) is still sufficiently large to contradict the image of a university as an internal safe haven.

A small number of fatalities is caused by people associated with one university who bring violence to one or more students from different universities. For example, in February 2007 in Tempe, Arizona, Joshua Mendel, a student at Collins College, committed suicide after fatally shooting Carol Kestenbaum (who was enrolled at Arizona State University) and Nicole Schiffman (a student from the University of Maryland who had come to visit Kestenbaum) because of something Carol said to a fourth person (Mendel's girlfriend; Garbe, 2007). Or there can be clashes between people (typically students) of different schools: As a case in point, one student was killed and five wounded in January 2002 when students from Catawba College and Livingston College clashed over a dispute that related to a party (Burchette, Weaver, & McCartney, 2002).

However, the principal perpetrators of fatalities are people who are not affiliated with any university. Sexual predators and thieves who find trusting university students good targets tend to add to this number.

Gender Factors

As might be expected, males tend to appear disproportionately among the list of perpetrators of, or accessories to, homicide. In fact, in the group of cases that pertains to single murders, despite the fact that there are some unknown assailants, 267 are accused male murderers. The number of males is somewhat inflated by gang activity; when there is a group of four, five, or six people involved in a killing, it is invariably a male group. In contrast, females are much more rarely murderers or accessories to murder: In the list of single homicides only 15 are females. Further, almost all the time, females act alone or in the company of a single friend or associate.

Among victims, males are slightly underrepresented, but not to any dramatic extent. Of 234 murdered members of the university communities, in cases involving single homicides, 114 were male and 120 were female.

One- and Two-Person Killings on Campus That Had the Potential to Turn Into Mass-Casualty Situations

While most of the murder cases that involved one or two slain people fall under the rubric of conventional crime, some cases that occurred on campus had the potential to turn into mass-casualty situations for the college or university. Beyond the Case Western Reserve case noted on p. 6, which resulted in one death and two injured, the following is of interest:

1. In 1979 Mark Houston, an 18-year-old barred from a fraternity party used a .32-caliber pistol to shoot seven students near the fraternity and on the grounds of the University of South Carolina. He killed two people and wounded five others. He was apprehended before he could cause further harm. The injured parties recovered (Violence in Our Schools, 1981–82).
2. In 1982 student Kelvin Love entered a computer classroom at Garland City Community College and fired his .357 Magnum at an instructor and a student, killing both. He then kidnapped a second student. There were other potential victims in the classroom and surrounding building, but Love did not continue his rampage (Violence in Our Schools, 1981–82).
3. In December 1983 nonstudent Su Young Kim invaded a Cornell University dormitory with a rifle and silencer and murdered his ex-girlfriend and her roommate. He held other students hostage for a time; the body count could have climbed, but Kim did not persist (Daniels, 2007).
4. In December 1992 at Simon's Rock College of Bard, Wayne Lo, an immigrant from Taiwan who was a scholarship recipient, armed with a cheap .22-caliber rifle, mortally shot a student and a professor and wounded four other students. His rifle jammed, ending the mayhem. Had he been better armed, used a heavier-caliber weapon, or had multiple guns at his disposal, more people might have been slain or wounded (Glaberson, 2000).

5. In February 2008 at Louisiana Technical College in Baton Rouge, female undergraduate Latina Williams entered a classroom with a semiautomatic pistol, shot and killed two female undergraduates she knew only superficially, then killed herself (Associated Press, 2008a).

In all these cases the presence of guns potentially raised the ante. Knifing, strangulation, and blunt force can be deadly to the individual, but for reasons of speed and efficiency they are not chosen methods if the goal is multiple deaths and injuries.

Multiple Murders

The initial temporal reference point of this study now shifts from the year 2000 to 1965 to look at the most serious set of cases, those that involve more than two killings (or multiple murders). This change in time frame also makes the analysis consistent with a point in history when there was a significant change in social and political mores, and the United States appeared to be more conflicted. When the focus is shifted from cases that involved one to two murders to those that were characterized by three or more deaths—for 1965 to 2008—more violence is seen on campus than off.

Four off-campus cases include the following:

> In January 1978 the infamous serial sexual-assault killer Ted Bundy murdered four female students and injured another at Florida State University. He committed his brutal crimes in three different locations, so it can be argued whether this represented one or more incidents, but the attacks occurred very close to one another in time and space and it is logical to see them as an extended event. The Florida case differs from earlier Bundy attacks in Washington and Oregon that were distinct single-person events conducted in a serial fashion at some distance in time and place (Bell, n.d.).

> In 1990 Danny Rolling, a less well-known but equally brutal serial sexual-assault killer, murdered four female students at the University of Florida, and a male student from a local community college who walked in on the scene of violence.

Again, given the closeness of the attacks in time and space, this is considered one extended event (Steel, n.d.).

➤ In May 1999 three students of Franciscan University were slain in their apartment by Terrel Yarbrough and an accomplice as part of a failed burglary (Pittsburgh Channel, 2000).

➤ In August 2007 three Delaware State University students were killed in Newark by Gerardo Gomez and others who may have been gang members in what appears to have been a sexual-orientation hate crime (Hurdle & Lee, 2007).

The number of on-campus incidents involving more than two murders (again excluding killers who committed suicide from the count) is shown in Table 1.7.

These multiple murders on campus can be divided into three subgroups: political events, workplace/academic conflict events, or mass-killer-status events.

Political events are associated with protests carried out in the late 1960s and early 1970s in relation to the civil rights and anti–Vietnam War movements. These include the following:

1. In February 1968, at South Carolina State University, officers with the highway patrol fired on a crowd that was protesting segregation at a nearby bowling alley. Three students were killed (including two from South Carolina State University), and 27 others were wounded (Brown, 2001).
2. At Kent State University in 1970, four students were killed and nine wounded when National Guardsmen opened up with rifle fire on people protesting the invasion of Cambodia. (A similar event

Table 1.7   Multiple Murders (> 2 Killed on Campus) Since 1965

Number of People Killed	Number of Incidents
3 people	4
4 people	1
5 people	1
6 people	1
7 people	1
> 7 people	2

took place at Jackson State University in the same year in which case two students were killed—including one student from Jackson State University—and 12 others were wounded; Caputo, 2005.)

Workplace/academic conflict events relate to professional, work, or academic contexts and include the following:

1. In 1976 at California State University at Fullerton, a custodian and former Marine, Edward Charles Allaway, opened fire with his .22 semiautomatic rifle in the school's film department, killing seven faculty/staff members who held diverse positions and wounding two others. He was motivated by the delusional belief that staff members in that department were compelling his estranged wife to perform as a sex slave in pornographic movies (Hardesty, 2006).
2. At the University of Iowa in 1991, Gang Lu, a Chinese graduate student who had successfully defended his PhD dissertation used .32- and .22-caliber handguns to slay three faculty members, one high level administrator, a clerical person, and a student because he felt he should have been awarded an extraordinary prize for his work (Marriott, 1991).
3. In August 1996 at San Diego State University, failing graduate student Frederick Davidson, using a 9 mm handgun, shot and killed three professors who had oversight of his troubled dissertation (Buto, 1996; San Diego college student, 1996).
4. In January 2002 Peter Odighizuwa, a 43-year-old law student from Nigeria who was having serious academic difficulties at the Appalachian School of Law, shot and killed an administrator, professor, and student, and injured three others (Bowman, 2002; Oliphant, 2002). According to one version of the story he was halted by several students who worked in police/security capacities outside school and who had access to weapons off duty, but another account indicates that the killer had expended his bullets and laid down his weapon when he lost the capacity to kill, and before he was actually apprehended (De Haven, 2009).
5. In October 2002 Robert Flores of Arizona State University, a Gulf War veteran, armed with a 9 mm pistol and a .357 revolver, killed three female professors whom he blamed for his academic difficulties in his nursing program before killing himself (Holguin, 2002).

Mass-killer-status events have three aspects:

1. They aim to produce a large number of casualties to create a mega incident that will give the killer lasting notoriety, a perverse major accomplishment, and a final justification for a wasted life.
2. The victims are chosen for logistical reasons, not because of a definable grievance (students and/or others in building X could serve as victims just as well as students and/or others in building Y).
3. The killer is bent on direct or indirect suicide (does not plan to survive this personal apocalypse).

At the university level, only three events are in this category. Table 1.8 summarizes their carnage; the three sections that follow offer additional commentary.

The Bell Tower Shooting at the University of Texas

In August 1966 Charles Whitman, a fair-haired 25-year-old former Marine from an upper-middle-class family, entered the bell tower at the University of Texas (Lavergne, 1998). Shortly before he had killed his wife and mother with knife thrusts to the heart while they slept to spare them the pain that would follow from the execution of his plan of terrorist action (Biography Project, 1999). Armed with several rifles, handguns, a knife, a hatchet, and a machete, he took up a barricaded sniper's position in the tower and fired down on the adjacent college town (Biography Project).

Table 1.8   Mass-Killer-Status Events

Institution	Year	Murdered	Wounded	Total Casualties	Fate of Killer
University of Texas at Austin	1966	15–17	30–31	46–47	Shot fatally by police
Virginia Tech University	2007	32	27	59	Suicide
Northern Illinois University	2008	5	21	26	Suicide

The loss of life was considerable in comparison to anything that had gone before and almost everything that has happened since in the shadow of a college campus. The number of deceased from the event (excluding the killer who was fatally shot by police) is sometimes reported as 15, but others have set it at 16 or 17 because an unborn child died at the time when a pregnant woman was shot, and an injured man passed away in 2001 from complications from the original wound and accordingly did not live out his natural life (Gamino, 2008).

The number of wounded was also very high, and it continues to stand as the highest number of injured for any single university shooting incident. Thirty to 31 individuals were reported injured (the number shifts slightly if the person who died in 2001 is tallied as deceased rather than wounded). With a total casualty count of 46 to 47, the event resembles more a day of war than a summer day on a college campus.

From the points of view of shock and morale, the university and town were devastated; however, in terms of student and faculty/staff fatalities, the outcome was less sanguinary than might be expected. Among the killed were two college students, one graduate student, a visiting professor, and a staff member. In fact, the majority of fatalities were nonuniversity personnel, including Whitman's wife and mother, three visitors to campus, a Peace Corps trainee, a local electrician, a city policeman, and two high school students.

Whitman, who had defined himself in opposition to an apparently brutal father who allegedly abused women and children, in the end killed his mother and his wife (Biography Project, 1999). He planned the subsequent mass slaughter, equipped himself with punctilious detail, and behaved without mercy to the people who cowered below; however, there were some redeeming qualities (Lisheron, 2001). At various stages in his life, Whitman labored to improve himself morally. Not long before the shooting, he sought help from a psychiatrist, explaining that he wanted to resist the impulse he felt to start shooting at people from the tower (Biography Project, 1999). He also wrote a last will of sorts and asked that any money he might have left at death go to support mental health causes, since he felt his own mental health was seriously compromised. Further, he complained frequently of terrible headaches and unsuccessfully sought medical help. Amphetamines and valium, which were prescribed to him, were probably not helpful. Finally, after his death he was found to have a cancerous brain tumor in the region of the amygdala, which may have undercut the efforts he made to maintain personal control (Biography Project).

Whitman deliberately sought to kill or wound a large number of people, and his assault was the conscious closing act of his life; however, he seems a more tragic than evil figure, for familial and physiological factors may have overwhelmed his own efforts to appeal to his better angel.

The Dual Shootings at Virginia Tech

On April 16, 2007, Seung Hui Cho, a 23-year-old senior one month shy of graduation—who was a permanent resident alien of Korean heritage—executed the bloodiest and most pitiless assault in the history of American higher education.[1]

Cho killed 32 university members, including 27 students. He also murdered five faculty members, including Professor Liviu Librescu, an elderly scholar, who had survived the Nazi Holocaust and who died a hero's death as he held a classroom door closed against the gun-wielding Cho. The good professor succumbed to Cho's gunfire, but not before he had bought precious seconds that allowed a number of students to escape through second-story windows (Downey, 2007).

In a poem, Cho referred to himself as a "loser" (Roy, 2009). He also labeled himself "Question Mark" in his writing and hid his face under a cap and reflective sunglasses—even indoors (Roy; Cahil et al., 2007). Diagnosed in secondary school with anxiety and depression (which were supposed to have abated) and selective mutism, his silence was broken on some occasions, such as when he spoke angrily to a professor (Sadock & Sadock, 2007). He also must have spoken with counselors and police at several points when he was required to answer questions to comply with legal and mental health obligations. Some would suggest that his mutism was at least partly manipulative, that it allowed him to show passively the disdain he felt for others, reduced the amount of work he needed to do for class, deflected unwanted attention, and permitted him to mask malevolent intentions that may have been from his middle school years (Shapira & Ruane, 2007). However, it is also undeniable that he had lifelong problems with even basic communication. Even with people he had known for very long periods of time—such as his parents—he seems to have spoken in rare, brief, and fragmentary sentences (Shapira & Ruane).

Cho began his studies in quantitative business-oriented areas. Despite communication issues that would tend to make a liberal arts major an unlikely choice, he decided to switch his major to English. Cho hoped to be a highly successful playwright and novelist, but the quality of works that he wrote and that have surfaced—*Richard McBeef, Mr. Brownstone*, and *The Adventure of Spanky*—indicate that his aspirations vastly exceeded his talent (Repository of Virginia Tech April 16 documents, 2007).[2]

Cho began his murderous spree on the morning of April 16, 2007. He entered a residence hall, West Ambler Johnston, and at about 7:15 a.m. executed a female student he almost certainly did not know (ABC News, 2007). In addition, he fatally shot a male resident assistant he also seems to have had no acquaintance with, who probably came to the scene to investigate a loud noise (the gunshot). After exiting the building, changing clothes, destroying personal effects, and going to the local post office to mail to NBC News what amounted to a self-promoting, in-praise-of-mass-murder press kit, he entered Norris Hall, a classroom building on the other side of campus. Having chained the three exterior doors so no one could escape the building, he opened fire at about 9:40 a.m., proceeding from classroom to classroom. In nine minutes, he created a horrific scene of pain, suffering, and death (Virginia Tech Review Panel, 2007).

In his middle school, Cho shared with school officials his admiration for and desire to imitate the killers of Columbine High School (these middle-school officials apparently did not pass on the information to anyone outside the junior high) (Virginia Tech Review Panel, 2007). However, unlike Dylan Klebold and Eric Harris of Columbine who held their fire for a few favored students, Cho spared no one. Armed with two semiautomatic handguns (a Glock 9 mm and a

Walther .22) and multiple 10- and 15-bullet clips, he had the capacity to produce a very rapid rate of fire, and he poured as many bullets into as many people as possible. In fact, he returned several times to individuals who had been shot to fire additional cartridges into their bodies. After expending close to 200 rounds in 9 minutes (while still retaining more than 200 bullets on his person), and with police closing in on him, he shot himself in the head. An autopsy showed that unlike Whitman there were no physiological brain irregularities that might have explained his unspeakable behavior (Rucker, 2007).

Cho was an equal-opportunity killer. Among the fallen were the old and young, wealthy and poor, male and female, African Americans, Hispanics, Caucasians, South Asians, East Asians, and people of Middle Eastern extraction. The victims were individuals from a wide variety of curricula, different schools, from many states and countries, and from many different religious and spiritual backgrounds. One of his victims was also of Korean extraction (Virginia Tech Review Panel, 2007).

There had never been a two-site shooting on a college campus. Why did Cho begin with a double killing in West Ambler Johnston, take a break to take care of several tasks including visiting the post office, and then engage in mass murder in Norris Hall? Some have theorized that the first foray was intentionally designed to create a diversion: Since the first attack resembled a domestic or acquaintance-based incident and took place on the other side of campus, it might have allowed him a freer hand for more generalized and anonymous terror in Norris Hall (Virginia Tech Review Panel, 2007).

A second assumption is that Cho was at least a relative failure in everything he did in his personal, family, social, academic, and professional life. He had no friends, had never held a job, and had limited future prospects. Graduation was rapidly approaching, which must have been terrifying for him. Cho had hoped he would become a successful writer, and he was bitterly disappointed when his first novel was summarily rejected by a publishing house some months before. After that rejection, he seems to have fallen back on an older personal narrative: It appears he believed that he could still leave his mark by doing for his university what his heroes, Klebold and Harris, had done for their high school (Virginia Tech Review Panel, 2007).

However, there was a kind of professional pitfall. It was just possible that Cho might not be able to kill; here too he could be a failure. However, early that morning, with a double murder under his belt, Cho knew that he could kill easily and efficiently. The shooting in West Ambler Johnston and the subsequent mailing of his self-promotional piece from the post office in all probability were preparatory acts 1 and 2. They laid the groundwork for the final act 3: the Götter-dämmerung in Norris Hall.

The Cole Hall Mass Shooting at Northern Illinois University

There was a triple irony in the events of February 14, 2008, at Northern Illinois University (NIU). The first irony was that on a day given over to love—or at least romantic love—Steven Kazmierczak, a recent alumnus who apparently was making a smooth transition from NIU to graduate study at the University of Illinois at Urbana-Champaign, entered a large classroom at his former campus and opened fire on a sizable number of students (Vann, 2008). First using a sawed-off shotgun to create fear and panic and then employing semiautomatic handguns (he had in his possession a Glock 9 mm, a Hi Point .380, and a Sig Sauer .38; Vann), he killed 5 students and wounded 21 others (20 students and 1 instructor; Boudreau & Zamost, 2008). The event stands as the second bloodiest event in the history of higher education in terms of the number of students killed and wounded. From the student perspective, only the event at Virginia Tech was worse.

The second irony is that the role model for Kazmierczak was not the villain who brought about a mass killing on an earlier St. Valentine's Day. His source of inspiration was not Alphonse Capone of the south side of Chicago. It was Seung Hui Cho of northern Virginia. As Cho had been inspired by Dylan Klebold and Eric Harris, so was Kazmierczak moved by the virtuoso killing performance of Cho (Vann, 2008).

The third irony was that immediately after the attack, Kazmierczak was described in laudatory terms. He had a loving fiancée, he had recently won a dean's academic prize, he was a dedicated tutor, and he had earned excellent grades by dint of hard work. He was accepted for graduate study at a distinguished Big Ten school, and his career prospects were solid. How could an accomplished student with a stable social life and sound professional prospects end up at this point (Davey, 2008; Fest, 2008)?

Closer investigation shows that Kazmierczak was extremely conflicted and that the recent facade of smooth accomplishment hid a deeply unstable core that had existed for many years. The complications included the following:

- He had prior diagnoses for depression, bipolar disorder, and obsessive-compulsive disorder. Various people had characterized his behavior as "paranoid" or "psychotic" (Associated Press, 2008b; Rice, 2008).
- Some years before, he had attempted suicide at least four times by overdosing and cutting his wrists.
- His medical treatment history features a pharmacopeia of legal drugs (e.g., Prozac, Depakote, lithium, Zyprexa, Paxil, Cogentin, Risperdal, Clozaril, Cylert, etc.). Kazmierczak frequently went on and off drugs for several reasons: to avoid side effects (weight gain, acne, or insomnia), to qualify for military service, and to address issues that arose from his being noncompliant with medication (when he became too unstable he would start taking it again; Boudreau & Zamost, 2008b).
- He used illegal drugs including marijuana and possibly LSD.
- He experienced early institutionalization in the Mary Hill Group Home during his high school years.
- His exposure to violent movies, music, and video games, including sniper games, was heavy.
- He had a problematic work record (trouble sustaining jobs earlier and at the end of his life).
- He was confused about his sexual orientation.
- His extreme promiscuity was mixed with intimate feelings for one person.
- A fascination with guns and explosive devices went back to his childhood.
- His discharge from the army was questionable (Davey, 2008).
- He had experience with a shotgun as a trainee in the field of corrections.
- Very disappointing scores on his LSAT truncated his plans for law school.

➤ His expressed admiration for Cho was complemented by his early interest in Ted Bundy, Jeffrey Dahmer, and Adolf Hitler.

The ultimate irony is that Steven Kazmierczak, the seemingly successful and untroubled graduate student, had a myriad of personal and psychological issues.

Some Comparative Aspects of the Three Mass-Murder-Status Killers

Whitman, Cho, and Kazmierczak differed from each other in a number of ways. One was of English stock, the second had an East Asian background, and the third had an Eastern European one. They lived in the Southwest, the Mid-Atlantic region, and the Midwest. One had a wife, another had never even been kissed by a female outside his family, and the third had a large number of casual sexual partners. One tried to resist mass murder, another embraced it completely, and the third was ambivalent.

They possessed several commonalities:

➤ First, they all were beyond the age of 21, supposedly the age of a stable adult, when universities should recognize personal autonomy, when parental responsibilities ought to be relaxed, and when one might surely have a rudimentary ethical code. (Whitman was 25, Cho was 23, and Kazmierczak was 27.) Particularly with Cho and Kazmierczak, and their sexual issues, the stated biological ages seem much in advance of their developmental ages. Cho, in particular, wrote like a 12- or 13-year-old.

➤ Second, they all used multiple guns, since they intended to, and did, generate large casualty totals (a knife or a six-shooter would hardly work for mass murder). Whitman received his training with weapons in the Marines, and Kazmierzcak had the benefit of weapons training in the military and in corrections; however, Cho was entirely self-taught. He purchased his weapons locally and from a dealer in Wisconsin, and he practiced at a range in a nearby town (Schaper, 2008).

▸ Third, they were prepared to die either by their own hands or at the hands of the police. Theirs was a no-exit game.

▸ Fourth, they hated "the other"—the other, at least at the end, being anyone who was not them. They were not bigots, they were misanthropes. They hated no specific individuals, groups, or causes; they hated life and humanity generally. The dead and dying had no significance to them; corpses were simply building blocks in a monument to personal vanity and infamy (Vann, 2008).

The Nexus Between Suicide and Homicide

It is difficult to tabulate an exact number of university students who commit suicide each year. Suicide tends to be kept private and is underreported since in many quarters it is still regarded as shameful, sinful, or socially embarrassing. It can also have adverse financial implications (e.g., no insurance benefits). In addition, sometimes the facts are unclear: Did the person who overdosed truly understand the dangerous interplay of several drugs taken together, or could the individual whose car collided with a tree simply have lost control of the vehicle?

If suicide is not completely quantifiable, and if it is apparently less frequent among university students than among noncollege peers, it is still all too common. With an estimate of 1,100 completed suicides a year among university students, it is generally characterized as either the second or third leading cause of death among this population (Potter, Silverman, Connorton, & Posner, 2004).

Looking beyond completed suicide and considering attempts and serious planning for fatal self-harm, the frequency increases. It is likely that nearly 10% of university students will seriously consider suicide in any particular year. If the baseline is fleeting ideation (e.g., caused by temporary discouragement in the aftermath of a romantic breakup or failed exam), then the number can become very large indeed (U.S. Department of Health and Human Services, 1999).

The number of suicides is much larger than the number of homicides, and the vast majority of people who are at risk for suicide represent a direct physical threat to themselves only. A very small minority decide intentionally to combine suicide with homicide; it seems that still fewer accidentally employ a method that unintentionally endangers others (e.g., turning on gas in a commonly occupied apartment without understanding the full implications). The harm that suicides do to others is generally more indirect and subtle (such as causing emotional distress among family, friends, and schoolmates).

In reviewing the murders of college students that are committed as part of a conventional criminal activity—escalated fighting, sexual assault, burglary, carjacking, and so on—suicide is almost never seen; however, suicide is more common in other instances.

First, suicide happens in cases where murder is spurred by obsession related to a real or imagined romantic/sexual relationship. For example, Kathleen Roskot, a sophomore at Columbia University in 2000, was killed by Thomas Nelford, a senior on leave from the same school, because their relationship was coming to an end. He dispatched her by knife, then threw himself under a subway train (Barton, 2000). At North Carolina State University in 2002, Lili Wang was gunned down on a campus tennis court by fellow graduate student Richard Anderson who then shot himself. Anderson seems to have had a largely platonic relationship with Wang but apparently was infatuated with her specifically and with Asian women in general (Chow, 2002). Finally, in October 2006 at the University of Central Florida, Nhat-Ahn Tran was knifed to death in her off-campus apartment by her nonstudent boyfriend, Loc Tran, before he attempted to commit suicide (Lundy, 2009).

Second, homicide/suicide appears in some cases in which the murder is caused by professional or academic conflict. Two examples of such cases include Professor John Locke of the University of Arkansas, who in 2000 was shot to death by his graduate student James Easton Kelly who had been dismissed from the program (University of Arkansas, 2000), and Jian Chen of the University of Washington, who, after being dismissed from his graduate program and facing return to China, shot his adviser, Rodger Haggitt, and then turned the gun on himself (KomoNews, 2006).

Among the three cases of mass-murder-status killers, technically, suicide did not apply to Charles Whitman. He was killed by police, not by his own hand. However, one might concede that he had put himself in a position (the top of a bell tower) that made escape—save by humiliating submission—impossible.

Cho and Kazmierczak were unambiguous suicides. There is some indication that Cho thought about possible escape scenarios (otherwise why would he have filed the serial numbers off his guns?); and Kazmierczak might have done as much also because he bought an engagement ring for the woman he was closest to just a few days before his rampage. However, in the end Cho and Kazmierczak seem to have preferred suicide for two reasons: From their vantage points, the quality of their lives probably seemed so bleak that death could constitute a relief, and the celebrity bathos they desired which would give a kind of retroactive meaning to their lives would be entirely undercut if they were to surrender.

Was suicide clearly foreseeable? Should people have known that Cho and Kazmierczak were at very high risk for suicide? In Cho's case, he had been subjected to a mandatory psychiatric review by the university's Community Services Board in 2005. He had been reprimanded in a measured way by school authorities for writing a rather pathetic and definitely unwanted (but not expressly threatening) note to a coed that "he might as well kill himself" (seemingly because of his social embarrassment). After having been seen and evaluated by the Community Services Board, he was given a temporary detention order that resulted in an overnight stay in a psychiatric hospital. An independent examiner and psychiatrist then reviewed his case, and in a subsequent hearing, a magistrate gave Cho a mandatory outpatient commitment order. Since the order was entrusted to the would-be patient himself and not to a mental health provider, the implication was that this did not appear to be a highly critical situation. In addition, Cho's brief and conditional statement of despair was not accompanied by additional indicators; for example, there was no indication in 2005 of a plan, timeline, or effort to obtain the means for suicide (Virginia Tech Review Panel, 2007).

Because Cho's suicide occurred in the context of mass homicide, it seems that the mental health board or the local magistrate should have gleaned that Cho was homicidal and suicidal. This makes too much use of hindsight. From the information available, it seems that no therapist or magistrate who saw Cho at the time viewed him as a danger to others.

Cho's situation also lacked *imminence*. Traditionally, when counselors speak of an imminent threat of suicide, they mean a time frame measured in hours or days. Although unknown at his university, Cho's attraction to suicide (and concomitant homicide) could be traced at least 8 *years* to middle school. Turning to his college years, fully 16 months passed between the magistrate's mandatory outpatient commitment order (because of concerns about suicidal ideation), and Cho's actual suicide/homicide. In the wake of Cho's heinous crime, an argument can be made for defining *imminent* in terms of weeks, months, years, or even decades. However, it is important to understand that prior to April 16, 2007, and even today, imminence is not normally defined in multiple months or years.

By contrast, Kazmierczak went beyond suicidal ideation to multiple actual attempts. In fact, he had tried to commit suicide four times, but those attempts occurred prior to his enrollment in college, and it does not appear that the attempts were known in the university environment. He did see a counselor at the University of Illinois at Urbana-Champaign where he was a new graduate student, but he never shared the desperation he felt (Vann, 2008). He apparently went to the counselor for the narrow purpose of obtaining certain medications for temporary use; he was not seeking in-depth treatment. As with Cho, there is no information to suggest that anyone saw Kazmierczak as a danger to others (Kaler, 2008).

In retrospect, could it be that universities, which offer great personal privacy and freedom, expect a modicum of personal discipline and self-control, and ought to balance the needs of the individual with the broader academic community were the precisely wrong places for Cho and Kazmierczak? Did these two really need more constant treatment, more long-term mental health care, more secure facilities, and more closely monitored medication? Were Cho and Kazmierczak the exceptions that prove the rule about the general efficacy of community mental health? In the end, did they really need the sort of long-term hospital or sanitarium care that hearkens back to a different age?

Heterogeneity in Murder Cases
Involving University Students

Homogeneity cannot be ascribed to cases of murder that pertain to the university population. There are individual murders, double murders, multiple murders, and in some very rare cases, mass murders. Homicide can be rooted in so-called common crimes, sexually predatory behavior, psychological conditions, workplace or academic conflict, discrimination, political action or reaction, and the desire to achieve lasting infamy, among other reasons. Murder can be heightened by anger, jealousy, despair, passion, prejudice, greed, vengeance, and so on. Murders of university students typically take place off campus, but sometimes they occur in remote locations, and because of iconic value, large-scale murderers are likely to choose central university facilities or landmarks for their stage setting.

Murder does not discriminate, either with respect to the murdered or to those who murder. Victims look like a cross sample of America —as seen in the list of assembled cases. As for murderers, their race and ethnicity include Caucasian, African American, Hispanic, Pacific Islander, East Asian, South Asian, and Native American, from the ranks of U.S. citizens but occasionally from international and undocumented backgrounds.

Turning to gender, women murderers are much less in evidence. Of the 262 single murder cases tabulated for the period 2000–2008, only 15 women took the lead or actively assisted in murderous activities; in the previous decade, there was one potential female mass shooter. In September 1996, near the student center at Pennsylvania State University, Jillian Robbins, dressed in fatigues and armed with a high-powered rifle, killed one student and injured another. Fortunately, she was disarmed by a Good Samaritan before she could do worse (Harris, 1997).

Beyond traditional demographic groups, people from unexpected backgrounds figure in the list of murderers. For example, one professor at a major university had murdered no fewer than three people when he was in his late teens (Smallwood, 2003). Another professor, William Slagle, the debate coach at Samford University, killed his student advisee, Rex Copeland, apparently because the student intended to quit the debate team and would not be dissuaded (Diehl, 2007). Undoubtedly most parents love and are supportive of their children in college, but at least one case stands in dramatic contrast: In September 2006 Douglas Pennington traveled to Shepherd University and shot to death his two boys, Logan and Benjamin, before turning the gun on himself (McMillion, 2007). Parents can even become involved in nefarious ways with roommates: In April 2008 at Purdue University, a roommate's mother fatally stabbed Liette Martinez with a knife (Daniels, 2008).

Because the matter of murder of university students is so heterogeneous, there cannot be a one-size-fits-all solution. In a single case of domestic or acquaintance-based violence in which the perpetrator is nonuniversity and has left the campus, it might be advisable to allow the police a modicum of time to analyze the situation and close in on the suspect before broadcasting alarms. However, if there is an indication of a mass shooter on campus, clearly an immediate and universal warning is critical.

At Virginia Tech, the situation was complicated by a conflict between illusion and reality. The initial double murder in the residence hall gave the illusion of domestic or acquaintance-based violence, which is not infrequent in the data on student murders, while in reality it was a preliminary skirmish to the slaughter that would take place later that morning in a classroom building across campus. Such a binary murder event had never occurred on a university campus. Focusing only on the mass murder part, there was an element of surprise because in April 2007 just one precedent existed for a broad attack on a university campus by a student of the university, and that was the University of Texas bell tower incident, which had taken place 41 years earlier. Further, that event was more an attack on the town and the town dwellers from a university perch; in many ways, it was not a focused attack on the university and its students.

It also must be conceded that if there can be binary combinations the Virginia Tech permutation is not the only one that may come into play. It is conceivable, for example, that rather than combining a situation that looks like domestic violence with a delayed attack on a classroom building, the former could be joined to an exterior sniper situation, such as at the University of Texas. In such a case, if prompt public warnings encourage people to leave campus and traffic jams result, the outcome could be an open line of fire on scores or even hundreds of people. In dealing with a two-shooter scenario as well as a dual setting, such as occurred with Klebold and Harris at Columbine High School, how much more complicated could the situation be?

A lot of faith has been placed in lockdowns; however, several problems are associated with them (Virginia Tech Review Panel, 2007). Lockdowns tend to be most workable in single-building institutions; in contrast, a lockdown is very hard if not impossible to effect in a timely way for an intermediate-size or large university that may have scores or even hundreds of buildings on a sprawling campus. Second, and especially on a large campus, how do administrators compel cooperation? Will staff forcibly prevent people from leaving or entering a room by saying "door locked" if a student outside the door pleadingly requests entry, even though that person could be a killer? In addition, if the killer is internal rather than external to the university, which tends to occur in mass violence incidents inside and outside the United States, there is the risk of locking many innocent people in with a cold-blooded murderer. Further, the internal killer would have access to all mass e-mails, text-messages, and voice-mails, so he or she would obtain more perfect intelligence from mass communication and could modify his or her attack plans to maximum effect.

The best chance for safety, which can never be truly guaranteed if a homicide/suicide killer is intent on making the university the target and will take his or her own life, does not rest in following a precise set of violence-prevention steps like a recipe in a cookbook, but in using one's coolness, courage, prudence, and analytical skill to make the best decisions under only partially known conditions. While few would countenance a lengthy delay in publicly reporting a murder, which apparently occurred at Eastern Michigan University in 2007 (Epstein, 2007), broadcasting pell-mell confused facts, undigested details, and ill-informed conjecture can produce panic, disorder, and unintended consequences, especially on large campuses. In mass shooting situations, the president of a university and his or her advisers somehow have to act, not like accomplished academic or business executives but rather as brilliant generals and adjutants on a battle-field. This is not an easy or enviable duty, but sometimes the force of circumstance compels as much.

Rara Avis or Frequent Bird of Prey

While the loss of life of any member of the university community even because of accident or illness is terribly sad and diminishes the community in some way, murder and suicide make a still more injurious impact for reasons related to morality and morale. Further, among murders, those that involve mass killings have a kind of mega tonnage yield. They can shake an institution and its people to their core, and impose personal, academic, financial, and emotional burdens unlike anything else.

Charles Whitman could be regarded as a distant harbinger of things to come, but the violence in 2007 and 2008 appears to be an importation of behavior previously seen only in high schools (Vossekuil, Fein, Reddy, Borum, & Modzeleski, 2002). In a way, Dylan Klebold and Eric Harris in 1999 begat Seung Hui Cho, and Seung Hui Cho in 2007 begat Steven Kazmierczak in 2008. For 2009 and 2010, is the memory of Steven Kazmierczak—at this moment—in a period of its own gestation among some other sad and troubled people at universities or those headed for universities? Will Kazmierczak be metaphorically infertile? Will he produce a single errant being? Or will he spawn a brood of malefactors?

Hopefully, steps taken in the name of vigilance will prevent such an occurrence or occurrences, or at least seriously mitigate them. However, the stakes are too great either to ignore or minimize the challenge. In this case, the commonplace that those who refuse to learn from history are condemned to repeat it has deadly implications.

Expressed and Actual Violence

If Cho and Kazmierczak, in their expression, had been peaceful and utterly nonviolent prior to the events of April 16 and February 14, there would be no cause in this chapter to explore a connection between expressed and actual violence.

However, in four of Cho's strange, obscenity-laced, and scatological written pieces that came to light after his death, violence is evident. In one play, *Richard McBeef*, the protagonist is a teenage boy (Cho?) who falsely accuses a kindly stepfather of sexual assault, berates him for his humble but honest employment, manipulates his mother into assaulting her husband, and ultimately causes his own accidental death by physically attacking his stepfather himself. In a second play, *Mr. Brownstone*, three students swear to "get" their math teacher, ostensibly because he robbed them of slot machine winnings. However, even before that theft took place, they despise him because he is old, suffers from constipation, deducts points for late or missed assignments, and routinely engages in unwanted anal sex with students sent to detention. Turning to a third piece, which Cho wrote and shared online with classmates, he commented on a prior conversation in their class, which he did not participate in, on cultural variations in eating patterns by saying the members of the class made him want to puke and should be damned to hell (Repository of Virginia Tech April 16 documents, 2007). And information has surfaced about a prose piece that Cho wrote about a young man and his girlfriend who think about engaging in a murder spree that would be more fun than tragic but who turn away from that act of mayhem in the end (Repository of Virginia Tech April 16 documents).

In turning to Kazmierczak, there is less written material, but the expression of violence is still disturbing. For example, at Halloween, a few months before his attack, Kazmierczak dressed up as the character Jigsaw from the *Saw* movies. He sported a tattoo of a sword on his arm, which he kept uncovered more and more as his dark mood deepened (Rice, 2008). He wore T-shirts that revealed at best a mordant sense of humor: A black pullover with white lettering had the word "Terrorist" and the picture of an AK-47 assault rifle emblazoned across the chest, and a second made fun of the assassination of President John F. Kennedy (in referring to the former president's funeral procession, the tagline was "I Love a Parade"; Vann, 2008).

Violent expression followed by mass murder can lead to the position that violent writing or expression should be met with suspension or dismissal. However, a zero-tolerance policy for violent writing or expression faces four major hurdles: artistic freedom, free speech, academic privilege, and false positives.

Although some might prefer the genteel stories of Jane Austen, violence has a place in literature. Peter Weiss's (1967) play on the Marquis de Sade, for example, which deals with issues of the Holocaust by creating dramatic conflict between a bloody autocrat of the French Revolution and the eponymous inventor of sexual sadism, is great art. Cho's *Richard McBeef* surely should be placed at the other end of the spectrum in terms of quality, but if violent expression was banned, both would be off limits.

A still more formidable barrier is the First Amendment. So-called university speech codes of the 1980s were inspired by laudable anti-discrimination goals, but they were struck down by the courts or severely amended by internal governance actions especially when applied to public institutions—like Virginia Tech and NIU (UWM Post Inc., 1991). To be sure, sanctioning action is appropriate if violent expression manifests itself in substantial harassment or directed threats, but the sort of generalized, fictitious, and basically off-screen violence in Cho's plays—before his eruption—does not provide firm grounds to proceed.

With respect to academic privilege, faculty members and students tend to have special protections when it comes to expression on university campuses. Faculty are supported by tenure and a supportive guild tradition in this area; students are given considerable leeway for developmental reasons (many feel students should be allowed some room for experimentation, mistakes, and teachable moments).

Groups can present problems as well. The best example here might be the current phenomenon of Humans vs. Zombies, an interactive, broadly based game of tag that was created earlier this decade and is played at dozens of universities. Scores of student participants are divided into the "living" and "living dead," and they try to "kill" each other in their own fashion. The putative Zombies metaphorically try to bite their victims (they actually touch rather than chew on others) to transform them into ghouls, and the designated Humans try to symbolically kill the "walking evil" (typically by hitting them with Nerf balls or marshmallows and not something that could hurt, such

as a paintball gun). If carefully controlled (registering the participants, having clear rules about the devices that can be used, limiting
times and places), these games can be made fairly safe.

However, there are still sources of concern. If this stylized form
of play—which is based on assassination at its core—becomes too
extensive, and if the rules change, it can lead to actual injury. In
addition, it can provide camouflage for malefactors, allowing them to
stalk and act under the cover of ritualized play. Third, if a university
has had a serious act of violence on campus, such games can retraumatize students who are in recovery. And finally, desensitization to
violence can occur through non-reality-based means—music, films,
video games, and so on—but there is something about putting the
exercises in real times and places that can transform them from being
a diverting pastime to a warlike maneuver, particularly if a troubled
individual or individuals are involved.

The Scale of Violence

In Peter Weiss's play (1964), the irony is that the more dangerous
person is not the Marquis de Sade, the vicious sexual sadist, but the
one-time political idealist and the leader of the French Revolution,
Jean-Paul Marat. De Sade murders singly, is ritualized in his killing
(to feed his twisted personal passion), and resists mechanization. On
the other hand, Marat kills on a massive scale, is detached about
killing (just everyday politics), and brings efficiency to mass murder
through use of the guillotine. Both are lacking in redeeming personal
qualities, but Marat is the much greater danger to society. He represents not individual killing but mass murder.

In looking at murders of university students, there are not a few de
Sades. Joseph Henry, who in 1986 sexually assaulted and murdered
Jeanne Clery, is a good example of a predatory individual murderer
(Clery & Clery, 2002). There is no doubt that he did great harm to
an individual of extraordinary promise, her family, and her school;
but as evil as Henry was, the harm he did cannot compare to the
broad-scale destruction spread by Cho. Cho wanted to harm not one

individual but an entire community. He did not take one life (as despicable as that would be); he murdered 32 and physically injured 27 others. When dealing with 59 direct casualties, there is a geometric, not a simple arithmetic, progression in personal, familial, and institutional suffering.

In writing about Marat and de Sade, Weiss (1964) was really thinking of neither; the unstated character on stage was Adolf Hitler. In truth, Der Führer was much worse, much more dangerous than even Marat. And so the question must be asked: In comparing Henry and Cho, is there a third, more monstrous, figure waiting in the wings?

The number of mass-killing events on campus—especially those by mass-murder-status killers—have been few in number to date. However, that is rather like saying that we have only had two world wars. Will the threat to campuses accelerate, especially if a successor in mass murder builds on the examples provided by Cho and Kazmierczak?

Will technology offer a future mass-murder-status killer better means to perform his or her craft over a greater killing field? When some states have legalized, or are in the process of legalizing, sawed-off shotguns, silencers, increasingly large ammunition magazines, and even fully automated machine guns, what kind of damage can the next mass-murder-status killer produce? If we encourage simulated assassination games in an age in which gun sellers produce semiautomated firearms in Froot Loops colors to make them look like toys or fashion accessories, what does that portend (Lisberg, 2008)? When will the pace and reach of communication over the Internet propel more capacity to make verbal and written threats to individuals or organizations (Bennett, 2007)?

Safety rests not in the blind use of technology, acceleration in firepower put at the disposal of the individual, absolute standards applied to the First Amendment, or indulgence of bad behavior in the name of consumerism. Safety rests in critical thinking, making distinctions based on reason, neither underreacting nor overreacting to challenges, and realizing that true security resides in preferring peace first and employing counterviolence only as a final resort.

Notes

1. The section on Seung Hui Cho and the events of April 16, 2007, represent the views of Richard J. Ferraro, and his views alone. Ferraro came to Virginia Tech only 3 months before April 16, never had direct or indirect contact with Cho, and has not had access to Cho's psychological records. He writes as a historian trying to reconstruct an explanation of a near contemporary historical event; he is *not* writing as a psychological authority. Further, he is not acting as a spokesperson for the administration or for any other person or entity at Virginia Tech, and therefore what is contained herein does not necessarily reflect the views of other faculty or staff members at Virginia Tech.

2. *Repository of Virginia Tech April 16 documents.* These documents have not been catalogued. They are found on a dedicated computer in the Newman Library on the Virginia Tech campus in Blacksburg. They are the property of the state of Virginia, and are not available online. This collection should not be confused with the 4/16 archive, found in special collections in Newman Library at Virginia Tech, which houses material related to the recovery from the events of 4/16.

References

ABC News. (2007, April 24). *Report: Cho hired an escort before rampage.* Retrieved from http://abcnews.go.com/US/VATech/story?id = 3071730&page = 1&CMP = OTC-RSSFeeds0312

Associated Press. (2008a, February 9). *Louisiana shooter's mom haunted by daughter's deadly campus rage.* Retrieved from http://www.foxnews.com/story/0,2933,330207,00.html

Associated Press. (2008b, April 19). *NIU gunman's essays reveal his alienation.* Retrieved from http://cbs2chicago.com/niushootings/Steven.Kazmierczak.NIU.2.703982.html

Barton, D. (2000, February 7). In the slaying of a Columbia student, mourning and mystery. *New York Times.* Retrieved from http://www.nytimes.com/2000/02/07/nyregion/in-the-slaying-of-a-columbia-student-mourning-and-mystery.html

Bell, R. (n.d.). *Ted Bundy, notorious serial killer.* Crime Library on TruTV, Chapters12–15. Retrieved from http://www.trutv.com/library/crime/serial_killers/notorious/bun dy/index_1.html

Bennett, J. (2007, December 17). What you don't know can hurt you. *Newsweek.* Retrieved from http://www.newsweek.com/id/74322

Biography Project: Charles Whitman: Biography, bibliography, links. (1999). Retrieved from http://www.popsubculture.com/pop/bio_project/charles_whitman_docs.html

Boudreau, A., & Zamost, S. (2008a, February 16). *CNN exclusive: Secret files reveal NIU killer's past.* Retrieved from http://www.cnn.com/2009/CRIME/02/13/niu.shooting.investigation/index.html

Boudreau, A., & Zamost, S. (2008b, February 20). *Shooter was taking a cocktail of 3 drugs*. Retrieved from http://www.cnn.com/2008/CRIME/02/20/shooter.girlfriend /index.html

Bowman, R. (2002, January 18). *A shocked town still grasps for answers*. Retrieved from http://johnrlott.tripod.com/apla2.html

Brown, L. M. (2001, March 1). *Remembering the Orangeburg massacre*. Retrieved from http://findarticles.com/p/articles/mi_m0DXK/is_1_18/ai_72607475/

Burchette, J., Weaver, J., & McCartney, J. (2002, January 27). Shooting stuns two college communities. *Salisbury Post*. Retrieved from http://www.salisburypost.com /2002jan/012702a.htm

Buto, J. (1996, December 27). Trial date set for SDSU triple murder case. *Daily Aztec*. Retrieved from http://www.thedailyaztec.com/2.7445/trial-date-set-for-sdsu-triple-murder-case-1.1167059

Cahil, P., Dedman, B., Handelsman, S., Johnson, A., Popkin, J., & Williams, P. (2007, April 19). High school classmates say gunman was bullied: Police say package sent to NBC news between shootings is of little use. *MSNBC*. Retrieved from http://www.msnbc.msn.com/id/18169776//

Caputo, P. (2005). *13 Seconds: A look back at the Kent State shootings*. New York: Penguin.

Centers for Disease Control and Prevention. (2008). *Understanding school violence: Fact sheet* [Electronic version]. Retrieved from http://www.cdc.gov/ncipc/dvp/YVP /SV_FactSheet.pdf

Chow, M. (2002, November 8–14). North Carolina shooting—Possibly bias related. *Asian Week*. Retrieved from http://www.asianweek.com/2002_11_08/news_lili wang.html

Clery, C., & Clery, H. (2002). *Campus Watch*, 8(1). Retrieved from http://www.sec urityoncampus.org/newsletter/v08i1.pdf

Columbine Review Commission. (2001). *The report of Governor Bill Owens' Columbine Review Commission*. Retrieved from http://www.state.co.us/columbine/Col umbine_20Report_web.pdf

Daniels, B. (2008, September 19). NMSU student's killer gets 60 years. *Albuquerque Journal*. Retrieved from http://www.abqjournal.com/abqnews/index.php? option=com_conten t&task=view&id=6984

Daniels, F. (2007, April 19). Alums recall 1983 C.U. murders. Retrieved from http:// cornellsun.com/node/23016

Davey, M. (2008, February 16). Gunman showed few hints of trouble. *New York Times*. Retrieved from http://www.nytimes.com/2008/02/16/us/16gunman.html? ex=1360818000&en=0cfa5bfbb3a34255&ei=5088&partner=rssnyt&emc=rss

De Haven, H. H. (2009). The elephant in the ivory tower: Rampages in higher education and the case for institutional liability. *Journal of College and University Law*, 35(3), 535, fn 142.

Diel, S. (2007, April 26). Coach who killed debater seeks parole Monday. *Birmingham News*. Retrieved from http://blog.al.com/spotnews/2007/04/coach_who_ killed_debater_will.html

Downey, K. (2007, April 17). Virginia Tech shootings: Liviu Librescu. *Washington Post*. Retrieved from http://www.washingtonpost.com/wp-srv/metro/vatechshoot ings/victim s/Liviu_Librescu.html

Fest, J. (2008, February 16). Steve Kazmierczak: The secret life. *Huffington Post*. http://www.huffingtonpost.com/jonathan-fast/steve-kazmierczak-the-sec_b_87031 .html

Gamino, D. (2008, August 3). *UT tower shooting survivor still grieves: Claire Wilson James survived Charles Whitman's bullet; the baby she carried did not*. Retrieved from http://www.www1967.com/Assets/pdf/UT-TOWER-SHOOTINGS.pdf

Garbe, D. (2007, February 20). Suburban man kills 2 women, then self in Arizona. *Aurora Beacon News*. Retrieved from http://cbs2chicago.com/westsuburbanbureau /Joshua.Mendel.Carol.2.335453.html

Glaberson, W. (2000, April 12). Man and his son's slayer unite to ask why. *New York Times*. Retrieved from http://partners.nytimes.com/library/national/041200ram page-killers.html

Hardesty, G. (2006, May 20). Shootings recall CSUF ordeal 31 years ago. *Orange County Register*. Retrieved from http://www.ocregister.com/articles/-41796—.html

Harris, A. (1997, September 17). One year later . . . university community members recognize HUB shooting anniversary. *The Digital Collegian*. Retrieved from http://www.collegian.psu.edu/archive/1997/09/09-17-97tdc/09-17-97d01-012.htm

Holguin, J. (2002, October 29). *4 dead in Univ. of Arizona shooting*. Retrieved from http://www.cbsnews.com/stories/2002/10/29/national/main527308.shtml

Hurdle, J., & Lee, J. (2007, August 29). Newark victims mourned at a campus in Delaware. *New York Times*. Retrieved from http://www.nytimes.com/2007/08/29/ nyregion/29memorial.html?ei = 5088&en = 69c305c285992ff3&ex = 1346040000 &adxnnl = 1&partner = rssnyt&emc = rss&pagewanted = print&adxnnlx = 125877 4067-QHbCf0fwVHDE3NRrGK1H4g

Jeanne Clery Disclosure of Campus Security Policy and Campus Crime Statistics Act, 20 U.S.C. § 1092(f) (1992).

Kaler, R. (2008). *Offender identified in NIU shootings*. Retrieved from http://news.il linois.edu/news/08/0215niu.html

Kropko, M. R. (2005, November 13). Man faces Ohio university shooting trial. *Washington Post*. Retrieved from http://www.washingtonpost.com/wp-dyn/con-tent/arti cle/2005/11/13/AR2005111300437.html

Larsen, R. (1980). *Bundy: The deliberate stranger*. Englewood Cliffs, NJ: Prentice-Hall.

Lavergne, G. M. (1998). *A sniper in the tower*. New York: Bantam Books.

Lisberg, A. (2008, September 27). Wisconsin gun dealer relishes role as Mayor Mike Bloomberg's nemesis. *New York Daily News*. Retrieved from http://www.nydaily news.com/news/2008/09/27/2008-09-27_wisconsin_gun_dealer_relishes_role_ as_ma-1.html

Lisheron, M. (2001, December 9). *A killer's conscience*. Retrieved from http://www .statesman.com/specialreports/content/specialreports/whitman/index.html

Lundy, S. (2009, August 11). Conflict leads to mistrial in UCF murder case. *Orlando Sentinel.* Retrieved from http://articles.orlandosentinel.com/2009-08-12/news/loc_1_loc-tran-anh-tran-nhat-anh

Marriott, M. (1991, November 3). Gunman in Iowa wrote of plans in five letters. *New York Times.* Retrieved from http://www.nytimes.com/1991/11/03/us/gun man-in-iowa-wrote-of-plans-in-five-letters.html?sec=health

McMillion, D. (2007, September 7). Bench is memorial to Shepherd University students slain by dad. *Herald-Mail.* Retrieved from http://www.herald-mail.com/?module=displaystory&story_id=173993&format=html

Nelson, P. (1994). *Defending the devil: My story as Ted Bundy's lawyer.* New York: William Morrow.

Oliphant, J. (2002, June 20). A tragedy compounded. *Legal Times.* Retrieved from http://74.6.239.67/search/cache?ei=UTF-8&p=Peter+Odighizuwa%2C+stop ped+by+gun&xa=1gE2j0BCEHCkK.HrArfhYw—%2C1259116515&fr=yfp-t-701&u=www. law.com/jsp/article.jsp%3Fid%3D1024078861416&w=peter +odighizuwa+stopped; plstop+stops+gun+guns&d=NVgX6929T1M0&icp= 1&.intl=us&sig=QNUJEa0eyQFwb2eKQ3Ii1w—

Piehl, K. (2008, April 28). *Detectives chase Smiley Face murder mystery.* Retrieved from http://abcnews.go.com/GMA/story?id=4738621&page=1

Pittsburgh Channel. (2000, August 30). *Herring gets life in Franciscan murders.* Retrieved from http://www.thepittsburghchannel.com/news/60143/detail.html

Potter, L., Silverman, M., Connorton, E., & Posner, M. (2004, October 21). *Promoting mental health and preventing suicide in college and university settings.* Washington, DC: U.S. Department of Health and Human Services. Retrieved from http://www.sprc.org/library/college_sp_whitepaper.pdf

Rainy day murders. (1969, August 8). *Time.* Retrieved from http://www.time.com/time/magazine/article/0,9171,941275-1,00.html.

Ramsland, K. (2004). *The Gallaudet murders.* Retrieved from http://www.trutv.com/library/crime/serial_killers/weird/gallaud et_murders/1_index.html

Rice, J. R. (2008, February 15). *Steven Kazmierczak: The hidden abandonment.* Retrieved from http://blog.itsallaboutabandonment.com/2008/02/15/understand ing-steven-kazmierczak.aspx?ref=rss

Roy, L. (2009). *No right to remain silent.* New York: Crown.

Rucker, P. (2007, April 23). No abnormalities found in Cho's brain. *Washington Post.* Retrieved from http://www.washingtonpost.com/wp-dyn/content/article/2007/04/22/AR2007042201418.html

Sadock, B. J., & Sadock, V. A. (2007). *Kaplan and Sadock's synopsis of psychiatry* (9th ed.). Philadelphia: Lippincott Williams & Wilkins.

Sanchez, C. (2007, fall). The big lie: Criminal cases exploited to attack blacks. *Intelligence Report, 127.* Retrieved from http://www.splcenter.org/intel/intelreport/article.jsp?aid=819

San Diego college student held in slayings of three professors. (1996, August 16). *New York Times.* Retrieved from http://www.nytimes.com/1996/08/16/us/san-diego-college-student-held-in-slayings-of-three-professors.html

Schwarz, T. (2004). *The hillside strangler: A murderer's mind* (3rd ed.). Fresno, CA: Linden Publishing.

Security on Campus. (2009). *Complying with the Jeanne Clery Act* [Electronic version]. Retrieved from http://www.securityoncampus.org/index.php?option = com_content&view = articl e&id = 271&Itemid = 60

Shapira, I., & Ruane, M. (2007, April 18). Student wrote about death and spoke in whispers. *Washington Post*. Retrieved from http://www.washingtonpost.com/wp-dyn/content/article/2007/04/18/AR200704180016 2.html

Slavit, M. (2008, December 3). Prosecutors argue DNA evidence puts Rios as murderer. Retrieved from http://www.connectmidmissouri.com/News/story.aspx?id = 230199

Smallwood, S. (2003, September 12). The price of murder. *Chronicle of Higher Education, 50*(3), p. A8.

Steel, F. (n.d.). *Savage weekend: Danny Rolling*. Retrieved from http://www.trutv.com/library/crime/serial_killers/predators/rolling/gain_1.html

U.S. Department of Education. (2007). *The campus security data analysis cutting tool*. Retrieved from http://www.ope.ed.gov/security/

University of Arkansas. (2000, August 30). Campus shooting tragedy. *Daily Headlines*. Retrieved from http://dailyheadlines.uark.edu/1229.htm

Vann, D. (2008, August). Portrait of the school shooter as a young man. *Esquire*. Retrieved from http://www.esquire.com/features/steven-kazmierczak-0808?src = rss

Violence in Our Schools. (1981–82). Retrieved from http://www.columbine-angels.com/School_Violence_1981-1982.htm

Virginia Tech Review Panel. (2007). *Mass shootings at Virginia Tech: April 16, 2007*. Retrieved from http://www.governor.virginia.gov/TempContent/techPanelReport .cfm

Vossekuil, B., Fein, R. A., Reddy, M., Borum, R., & Modzeleski, W. (2002). *The final report and findings of the safe school initiative: Implications for the prevention of school attacks in the United States*. Washington, DC: U.S. Secret Service and U.S. Department of Justice.

Weiss, P. (1964). *The persecution and assassination of Jean-Paul Marat as performed by the inmates of the Asylum of Charenton under the direction of the Marquis of Sade*. London: J. Calder.

2 The Emotional Health and Violence Connection

Prevention, Intervention, and Resiliency

Courtney Knowles and Gwendolyn Jordan Dungy

IN THE aftermath of tragedies such as those at Virginia Tech and Northern Illinois University, there has been much discussion about the connection between mental health and campus violence. Both of those tragedies were mass killings that ended in suicide, and both shooters had histories of mental health problems. There is a definite correlation between mental illness and school shootings, but the realities of this connection and how it translates into preventing violence while protecting the emotional health of the larger student population is sometimes misunderstood. As colleges and universities across the country work to create or expand programs and policies to prevent violence on their campuses, it is important to understand the link between mental health and violence prevention and how this knowledge can improve the health and safety of the entire campus community.

There is an overwhelming connection between suicide and mental illness. Ninety percent of all people who die by suicide have a diagnosable psychiatric disorder at the time of their death (Goldsmith, 2002). Mental illness also plays a role in many mass killings. However, most of the emotional disorders that students struggle with do not lead to violence toward others, and overall students are more likely to die by harming themselves than by murder (National Mental Health Association & Jed Foundation, 2002). While it is important to realize that mental illness often plays a role in violent acts, it is equally important to remember that most students dealing with a mental health problem will never become violent (Elbogen & Johnson, 2009). Any action by a campus that creates a visible link between emotional disorders and violent behavior could worsen the stigma of mental illness and create barriers to seeking help for students concerned about their emotional health.

Since creating programs solely to prevent violent behavior by addressing mental health might worsen the stigma and prevent students from seeking help, it is most effective to make sure a school's efforts on violence prevention, suicide prevention, and mental health promotion are coordinated to complement each other and to streamline information to make it most likely that students at risk for self-harm *or* violence toward others are identified so the proper intervention can take place. A comprehensive mental health promotion and suicide prevention plan should be twofold. First, a campus-wide system of communication for collecting information about distressing or disturbing behavior by students should be created, and second, this information should be funneled to a central point. One tool for developing these policies and protocols, the Jed Foundation's (2006a) *Framework for Developing Institutional Protocols for the Acutely Distressed or Suicidal College Student*, is discussed in more detail on p. 43.

Mental health promotion and suicide prevention are also an important part of creating resiliency to aid in the response and recovery after tragedies such as school shootings. Research has shown that students most affected emotionally by campus tragedies are those who were previously distressed or had prior mental health conditions (Hughes et al., 2008). The same campus-wide plan that can identify students at risk of causing harm to themselves or others can also help connect distressed individuals to some kind of support, thereby creating a safety net that could be essential should they encounter a significant stressor like a campus shooting.

Whether as a means to prevent violence or to increase resiliency after a campus tragedy, a comprehensive plan for mental health promotion and suicide prevention cannot be overlooked when developing a method for protecting students from the devastating impact of campus violence.

College Mental Health: A Growing Concern

In general, the mental health of students is a growing concern for colleges and universities. A 2007 survey showed that 91.5% of counseling center directors reported an increasing number of students with severe psychological problems on their campuses, and that nearly half of their student clients had severe psychological problems (Gallagher, 2007). In a 2008 national survey of college students

> ➢ 13% had been diagnosed with a mental health condition
> ➢ 16% said they had a friend who talked about wanting to end his or her life during the last year
> ➢ 11% said they had a friend who had made a suicide attempt during the last year
> ➢ 9% had seriously considered suicide themselves during the last year

Of those who had considered suicide, only 40% had reached out for help from a counselor or professional (mtvU & Associated Press, 2008).

With earlier diagnosis and better treatments available, more students dealing with emotional disorders are now able to complete high school and successfully enter and complete college. Today's student mental health services are faced with at least three categories of students with major mental health conditions: those coming to campus already diagnosed and actively seeking continuing treatment, those who develop major mental illnesses while enrolled, and those who decide to forgo further treatment once enrolled and who subsequently relapse.

It is clear that students perceive campus life as stressful. Over half of today's students say they have been so stressed at some point during the last semester that they couldn't get their work done or didn't want to see friends (mtvU & Associated Press, 2008). For students dealing with existing or developing emotional disorders, the stressors of college life can lead to distress and interfere with their ability to function. Some are in various stages of recovery, while others lack the resiliency to confront the stresses and strains of campus life.

Moreover, certain groups whose numbers are growing on campuses—among them returning veterans, older nontraditional students, and international students—may have even greater stressors because of the complexity of their life experience in addition to school. For example, isolation and cultural and language barriers may put international students at higher risk for distress or suicidal ideation.

While students with emotional disorders or those lacking coping skills can excel in the college environment with the proper support, treatment, and/or lifestyle changes, it is important to recognize that they may be more susceptible to distress or conditions such as post-traumatic stress disorder (PTSD) after events such as campus violence. With the growing trend of students with mental health problems on campus, it is critical to acknowledge that creating a safety net for these individuals is an essential part of building campus-wide resiliency and protecting a student body against violence or other campus tragedies.

Mental Health and Violence

A study by Blanco et al. (2008) found that the predicted probability of violence in the case of severe mental illness alone is about the same as it is for subjects without severe mental illness. Individuals with severe mental illness and substance abuse and/or dependence were at a higher risk than individuals with either of these disorders alone. Individuals with dual disorders and a history of violence showed almost 10 times a higher risk of violence when compared to those with only severe mental illness. Historical, dispositional, and contextual factors, not mental illness, were the strongest predicators of future violence. The connection between mental illness, substance abuse, and violence is important to note, since research has shown that the risk of alcohol use disorders was significantly higher among college students than among their non-college-attending peers. Over 20% of college students met the criteria for alcohol use disorders (Blanco et al.).

A pilot study released in 2009 by the Center for the Study of Collegiate Mental Health (CSCMH) at Pennsylvania State University looked at data on students who used counseling services at 66 colleges or universities. CSCMH examined the data as it related to students who agreed with the statement, "I am afraid I may lose control and act violently." While agreeing with this statement is different than actually committing violent behavior, the expression of these fears could be an indicator of risk. The data showed that students with strong fears of losing control and acting violently were most likely to be male and to have previously harmed someone. They also indicated a likeliness of experiencing the following: fear of having a panic attack in public, unwanted thoughts that cannot be controlled, nightmares or flashbacks, irritable feelings, suicidal ideation, low academic motivation, and getting into arguments frequently (CSCMH). As Laker (2009) has asserted, "There is a need for thoughtful discussion about the social conditions, especially relating to identity development, which tolerate, dismiss, glamorize, or otherwise encourage such violence" (p. 1). While this data is not definitive enough to be used for screening, it does highlight some characteristics to be kept in mind when identifying and addressing students who could be at risk for violence.

Lessons From Virginia Tech: The Importance of Connection and Support

In 2007 the Jed Foundation provided funding for research conducted by Virginia Tech and Ronald Kessler of Harvard Medical School on the mental health needs of Virginia Tech students and faculty in the aftermath of the events of April 16, 2007. Over 4,600 students and 1,650 faculty members responded to the survey—a rate of about 20%. Data from the preliminary report revealed two key themes that could help other campuses best prepare for unexpected tragedies among their student population:

1. *The data show that those who were experiencing psychological distress before the shooting were at greater risk for distress after the shooting.* This means a critical part of creating a campus that can be resilient after a tragedy is connecting students struggling with

emotional issues to campus resources to improve coping skills and to provide a channel of support in the aftermath of traumatic events (Hughes et al., 2008).

2. *The data show that while over 25% of students either met criteria for or qualified as "possible" for PTSD, only 10% received some type of therapy or professional counseling.* Of those who did not receive any mental health services, 25% said they were unsure where to go or whom to see, 31% said they were embarrassed or worried about people knowing they were getting mental health help, and 25% did not think treatment would work. Raising awareness of a school's counseling services, decreasing the stigma of seeking help, and raising awareness of mental illnesses as treatable conditions could all be critical in ensuring that students struggling with potentially dangerous emotional issues such as PTSD after a traumatic event are most likely to reach out for support (Hughes et al.).

The comprehensive approach to promoting mental health and preventing suicide described in the following section addresses both these critical factors: increasing the likelihood that students with existing problems will be connected to support before a tragedy, and raising awareness in the student population about mental health issues and campus resources so they are more able and willing to get help after a crisis.

Emotional Health Safety Net: The Prescription for Prevention and Resiliency

As presented at the beginning of this chapter, a comprehensive campus plan for promoting mental health and preventing suicide is an essential part of violence prevention for three primary reasons:

1. Systems designed to identify and address students at risk for self-harm can also lead to intervention for students who may be at risk of harming others.
2. Despite best efforts, the possibility of violence can never be fully removed, so schools must also work to create the most resilient

campus populations to lessen the emotional harm that violence or other tragedies will have on the student body.
3. The more students and faculty understand about mental illness, the more likely they will be able to support peers dealing with emotional issues and recognize those who may be at risk of harming themselves or others.

The Jed Foundation (2006b) and the Suicide Prevention Resource Center, national organizations working to reduce emotional distress and prevent suicide among college students, have developed *Prescription for Prevention: A Model for Comprehensive Mental Health Promotion and Suicide Prevention for Colleges and Universities*, which has been used by institutions of higher education across the country to address and support distressed and at-risk students. The following are some key components of that model that support violence prevention efforts:

1. *Identify students who may be at risk for suicide or violent behaviors through the use of outreach efforts, screening, and other means.* This may include asking questions about mental health on students' medical history forms, voluntary screening programs, educating faculty and students to recognize and refer potentially high-risk individuals, and increasing coordination between campus disciplinary processes and mental health services. A key part of this process is the creation of a case-management committee, a threat assessment group made up of campus professionals from various disciplines to process information about potentially distressed students and to take appropriate action if necessary. After the latest high-profile cases of campus violence, many people have reported disturbing behavior. Having a central hub to process information on potentially at-risk students lessens the likelihood that recurring behavior will go unnoticed and unaddressed.

2. *Educate students about mental health and wellness, and encourage them to seek appropriate treatment for emotional issues.* According to the 2007 National Survey of Counseling Center Directors (Gallagher, 2007), only 20% of student suicides involved former or current clients, suggesting that counseling may be a protective factor

against suicide and that only a fraction of the students who need such help are seeking it (Gallagher). Therefore, it is essential to create campus communities that encourage seeking help by decreasing the stigma surrounding mental illness and raising awareness of available resources. If getting students who are struggling with emotional disorders connected to support is a key part of resiliency, then educating students about the signs and symptoms of mental illness and suicide should be a campus priority that extends far beyond the counseling center's walls. Strategies must be put in place across the campus community so that students receive messages in unexpected and nonthreatening places. Providing online self-assessment tools and information on helping a peer is also an effective way to identify and address mental health problems on campus.

3. *Create policies and procedures that promote the safety of distressed or suicidal students, and outline how to respond to crises including suicidal acts.* When students dealing with mental health problems become suicidal and/or violent, the campus response must be planned and carefully executed. Every school should have policies and procedures for responding to suicide attempts and high-risk behaviors, as well as a comprehensive disaster and follow-up plan. Many colleges have found the Jed Foundation's (2006a) *Framework for Developing Institutional Protocols for the Acutely Distressed or Suicidal College Student* to be a valuable blueprint for the development or revision of crisis procedures.

4. *Increase access to effective mental health services that accurately diagnose and appropriately treat students with emotional problems.* Colleges and universities should work to improve counseling services, team with other organizations in the community that focus on mental health issues, and train counseling center staff members to provide the best support to students, especially those who may be at risk for suicide or dangerous behaviors. This also involves educating campus mental health professionals on issues related to students' rights, confidentiality, and what to do if they are concerned about the safety of a client or others.

It is also important for colleges to realize that having strong mental health services in place is not the answer for all students. Those from cultures or backgrounds that do not understand or acknowledge mental illness or that discourage revelations of personal problems are not likely to seek services. In fact, less than 25% of students say that they would be likely to seek help if they were struggling emotionally (Jed Foundation & mtvU, 2006). Too often, institutions have created a culture of passive incident management, leaving less time to take proactive steps. Rigid systems and processes are reactive by nature and "often lack the proactivity to prevent potential danger or misconduct" (Lake, 2009, p. 17). Instead, colleges need to develop creative approaches to respond to those students in ways they will find helpful and nonthreatening.

5. *Promote social networks that reinforce a sense of campus community and relationships among students.* Colleges should work to reduce student isolation and encourage feelings of belonging. It is not simply a matter of urging each student to get involved but of creating opportunities in an environment of caring and connection. Student engagement not only enhances learning and development but is also one of the most important ways in which students develop a sense of connectedness and belonging within their campus community (Harper & Quaye, 2008). Such relationships can be significant protective factors against depression and suicide. This type of connection can also be important to resiliency should students be exposed to a traumatic event on campus.

6. *Help students develop life skills to face challenges.* Colleges should encourage and create programs that improve students' management of the rigors of campus life and equip them with the tools and techniques to manage triggers and stressors. Colleges should evaluate how the entire college experience provides opportunities to learn life skills that are appropriate for the developmental stage of traditional college students—not quite adults, no longer just adolescents—as well as adult learners whose skills could be more fully developed. A key component of these life skills is the ability and willingness to ask for help if needed, especially in relation to extreme trauma or tragedy.

7. *Restrict access to potentially lethal sites, weapons, and other agents that may facilitate suicide attempts.* Such actions might include

limiting access to roofs of buildings; replacing windows or restricting the size of window openings; denying access to chemicals, such as cyanide, that are often found in laboratories; prohibiting guns on campus; and controlling the use of alcohol and other drugs.

Developing a comprehensive institutional plan that incorporates these elements requires "presidents and senior officers in both academic and student affairs [to] adopt a partnership model that expects and rewards collaborations" (Keeling, 2004, p. 29) campus-wide across many departments and functional areas. Creating this collaboration can sometimes be challenging, but the resulting system can decrease the likelihood that a potentially suicidal or dangerous student will go unnoticed and increase the capacity of students and the campus community to be resilient in the aftermath of traumatic events such as campus violence. Institutions should also "establish routine ways to hear students' voices, consult with them, explore their opinions, and document the nature and quality of their experience" (Keeling, p. 28).

The Emotional Health and Violence Connection: Taking Action on Your Campus

Regardless of the size or demographic of your campus, here are some key questions to ask yourself and other campus stakeholders about the wellness and safety of your campus:

1. Are the violence prevention and mental health efforts on campus coordinated? Is there communication between the two efforts to make sure all students are as protected and supported as possible?
2. Are all campus professionals aware of the system for reporting information about students who may be in distress or at risk for harming themselves or others? If so, is the information collected through this system reviewed and acted on if necessary?
3. Is there a comprehensive plan for mental health promotion and suicide prevention on campus? Does it include efforts and outreach to help increase the likelihood that students with

emotional conditions are connected to support and know where to go for help if they are concerned about themselves or a peer?

If the answer to any of these questions is no, it is imperative to use available resources, such as those provided by the Jed Foundation and the National Association of Student Personnel Administrators, to put these systems, policies, and procedures in place to make sure violence prevention, mental health promotion, and suicide prevention strategies are coordinated to best protect the physical and emotional health of the campus community.

Conclusion

While it is imperative to remember that most students with mental health concerns will never pose a risk to others, it is in the best interest of the campus community to have systems in place that will increase the likelihood that students at risk for any type of dangerous behavior are identified and addressed. Comprehensive campus-wide efforts to provide a safety net for all students are essential to create safer campus communities and to ensure the greatest possible student success across the entire spectrum of mental health concerns—from handling typical college stressors to managing emotional disorders to coping with tragedies. Supporting the emotional health of students and preventing harmful behavior cannot be seen as the purview of a single campus department but must be the responsibility of all. Campuses must go through a strategic planning process and provide information and training to all campus stakeholders—faculty, staff, students, and administrators alike. It is important that campus administrators understand the needs of their students and the historical, dispositional, and contextual factors at play in their lives. Reducing the stigma of mental illness, providing support and services in nontraditional and nonthreatening ways, and actively involving students in prevention and intervention efforts is not only a critical part of preventing distress, suicide, and violence, but it is also a core responsibility of colleges and universities in protecting students' health and increasing the likelihood of their success during their college years and beyond.

References

Blanco, C., Mayumi Okuda, W. C., Hasin, D., Grant, B., Liu, S., & Olfson, M. (2008). Mental health of college students and their non-college-attending peers. *Archives of General Psychiatry, 65*(12), 1429–1437.

Center for the Study of Collegiate Mental Health. (2009). *2009 pilot study: Executive summary.* University Park: Pennsylvania State University.

Elbogen, E. B., & Johnson, S. C. (2009). The intricate link between violence and mental disorder: Results from the national epidemiologic survey on alcohol and related conditions. *Archives of General Psychiatry, 66*(2), 152–161.

Gallagher, R. (2007). *National survey of counseling center directors.* Alexandria, VA: International Association of Counseling Services

Goldsmith, S. P. (2002). *Reducing suicide: A national imperative.* Washington, DC: National Academies Press.

Harper, S., & Quaye, S. (2008). *Student engagement in higher education: Theoretical perspectives and practical approaches for diverse populations.* New York: Routledge.

Hughes, M., Jones, R., Kessler, R. C., Fairbank, J. A., Pynoos, R. S., Steinberg, A., et al. (2008). *Mental health needs assessment in the aftermath of the April 16 events at Virginia Tech: A brief preliminary report.* Blacksburg, VA: Virginia Polytechnic Institute and State University.

Jed Foundation. (2006a). *Framework for developing institutional protocols for the acutely distressed or suicidal college student.* New York: Author.

Jed Foundation. (2006b). *Prescription for prevention: A model for comprehensive mental health promotion and suicide prevention for colleges and universities.* New York: Author.

Jed Foundation & mtvU. (2006). *College mental health study: Stress, depression, stigma and students.* Retrieved from http://www.halfofus.com/_media/_pr/mtvu CollegeMentalHealthStudy2006.pdf

Keeling, R. (Ed.). (2004). *Learning reconsidered: A campus-wide focus on the student experience.* Washington, DC: National Association of Student Personnel Administrators and American College Personnel Association.

Lake, P. F. (2009). *Beyond discipline: Managing the modern higher education environment.* Bradenton, FL: Hierophant Enterprises.

Laker, J. A. (2009). What should we be doing to reduce or end campus violence? *Journal of College & Character, 10*(4). Retrieved from http://www.collegevalues .org/pdfs/laker.pdf

mtvU & Associated Press. (2008). *New mtvU and Associated Press poll shows how stress, war, the economy and other factors are affecting college students' mental health.* Retrieved from http://www.halfofus.com/_media/_pr/mtvU_AP_College_ Stress_and_Mental_Health_Poll_Executive_Summary.pdf

National Mental Health Association & Jed Foundation. (2002). *Expanding the safety net: Proceedings from an expert panel on vulnerability, depressive symptoms, and suicidal behavior on college campuses.* Alexandria, VA: National Mental Health Association.

U.S. Public Health Service. (2001). *National strategy for suicide prevention: Goals and objectives for action.* Rockville, MD: U.S. Department of Health and Human Services.

3 Managing the Whirlwind

Planning for and Responding to a Campus in Crisis

Brandi Hephner LaBanc, Thomas L. Krepel, Barbara J. Johnson, and Linda V. Herrmann

As UNIVERSITIES struggle to adapt to the changing demands associated with campus emergency planning and management, much of the initial effort goes into defining what it is that institutions are anticipating. Terms such as *crisis, disaster, emergency,* or *critical incident* are often used as the focal point of the planning effort. Surprisingly, although these terms are commonly used synonymously and interchangeably, there are major distinctions in the definitions of each. For example, a crisis or critical incident is typically defined as a turning point, an event of decisive importance with respect to an outcome, attended with risk or hazard. An emergency, on the other hand, is any sudden, urgent, unforeseen occurrence requiring immediate action. Disaster is defined as a sudden, calamitous event causing great damage, loss, or destruction. Some definitions abandon conceptual characteristics and use official acts (e.g., presidential declaration) or magnitude of the event (e.g., minor, major, severe) to operationalize terms such as emergency or crisis. Acts of violence on college and university campuses can exhibit some or all the elements of the various terms used in emergency planning and management. For example, mass shootings such as those at Virginia Tech (April 2007) and Northern Illinois University (February 2008) were decisive events that altered the character of each institution; they were unforeseen, sudden, required immediate response, caused great loss, had disastrous proportions, and triggered official declarations of disaster or emergency conditions.

Some might argue that it makes little difference what terminology is used, but close examination of the definition of each term suggests more than an immediate response and illuminates the longer-term effects on institutional culture and operations. Varying degrees of involvement and magnitude associated with emergency scenarios have a bearing on the planning, training, and response to such situations, while crisis or disaster conditions should be understood as likely to have a profound, long-term, culture-changing impact on the institution. To that end, this chapter outlines essential planning details, and we are especially mindful of the role of student affairs during campus crisis response. Particulars related to university-wide emergency plans, the related crisis response teams (CRTs) led by student affairs, and victim liaison programs are provided. Additionally, key aspects of communication during a crisis are explored, and recommendations are made regarding the management of information while responding to a crisis.

Violent acts in the academy, particularly where the act seems random and involves multiple casualties, can best be characterized by the term crisis. Response to such events requires not only advance planning and training but immediate action to halt or mitigate loss; furthermore, it has the potential for long-term effects on the campus community.

Planning for and Responding to Crisis

Campus Emergency Operations Plan

The events of September 11, 2001, led to major changes in how public and private organizations, including colleges and universities, plan for and respond to emergency situations. One result of the September 11 attacks was the issuance of Homeland Security Presidential Directive 5 (HSPD-5; see http://www.fas.org/irp/offdocs/nspd/hspd-5.html), which mandated the use of a national standard emergency management system. The National Incident Management System (NIMS) is the basis that most colleges and universities today use for constructing their emergency response plans. University administrators should become familiar with NIMS and NIMS-compliant emergency operations planning in order to fulfill responsibilities for emergency preparation and to comply with statutory requirements. For example, the federal Higher Education Opportunity Act (2008), which applies to virtually every university in the United States, mandates certain emergency planning and disclosure actions that include adopting and publishing an emergency response policy, conducting annual emergency response drills, and using electronic media for communication under emergency conditions.

NIMS provides a template for establishing structures and processes for emergency planning and response (U.S. Department of Homeland Security, 2007). Because NIMS is a national template, it is portable and facilitates communication and coordination among and across agencies and organizations that can be called upon in emergency situations. NIMS-compliant plans typically are referred to as emergency operations plans (EOPs; U.S. Department of Homeland Security; International Association of Campus Law Enforcement Administrators [IACLEA], 2007). A university EOP, if NIMS compliant, will provide a command structure and assignments of responsibility and authority; a concept of operations focused on mitigation, preparedness, response, and recovery; and a series of annexes or appendixes that address specific emergency response functions such as communication and warning, fire and rescue, public information, evacuation, and the emergency operations center (EOC). NIMS-compliant EOPs are intended to be based on all-hazard planning, which can include but is not limited to weather emergencies, civil disturbance, acts of violence, or hazardous materials incidents (U.S. Department of Homeland Security).

The EOP is an essential institutional planning and management document that should be available to all executive-level administrators and other relevant personnel (U.S. Department of Homeland Security, 2007; IACLEA, 2007). Periodic training under the EOP is critically important for many reasons. Appropriate training activities allow designated individuals to know their assignments and to perform those duties under simulated conditions. Training activities provide an opportunity to field-test the EOP and collect valuable insights on how the plan can be adapted to the specific environment and culture of the university. EOP training activities present the opportunity to involve outside agencies that may be called upon in large-scale events, thus fostering understanding of protocols and positive working relations. Of critical importance, training under the EOP allows the broad range of personnel involved in emergency response to understand the use of the incident command system, another common feature of the EOP (U.S. Department of Homeland Security).

A NIMS-compliant EOP makes a critical distinction between the incident command post (ICP) and the EOC, a distinction that should be understood and practiced by campus administrators (U.S. Department of Homeland Security, 2007). The ICP is the on-site location for response to and management of the emergency situation. The ICP is led by the incident commander (IC). An ICP/IC can respond to a range of incidents that vary in severity; typically, those conditions fall into the categories of minor, major, and disaster conditions. Although an ICP/IC can be designated and established for any emergency situation, it is not until a situation rises to the level of a major emergency or disaster that the organizational EOC is activated (U.S. Department of Homeland Security).

While the ICP/IC is on site, the EOC is staffed by designated institutional personnel who typically carry executive-level administrative responsibilities (e.g., president, vice president; U.S. Department of Homeland Security, 2007). The ICP/IC can be located anywhere, depending on the incident, whereas the EOC is located at a designated site on campus. Typically, an institutional EOP will specify who has the authority to activate the EOP; a first responder (e.g., campus police officer) dealing with a minor emergency may activate selected elements of the EOP without engaging institutional-level administrative officers or activating the institutional EOC. But as incidents escalate in seriousness, the activation of the EOP and the EOC tends to move to higher institutional authority including the chief security officer and president. Incidents that fall into the major emergency or disaster category will almost invariably trigger activation of the EOP and EOC.

It is critically important to understand the distinction between the ICP/IC and the EOC. Response to a particular situation is the responsibility of the IC who uses the resources at his or her disposal. It is not the role of EOC personnel to try to substitute for the ICP/IC. Rather, the role of the EOC is to address ongoing institutional operations and to provide strategic policy oversight of the emergency situation. The role of the ICP/IC is tactical, while the role of the EOC is strategic (IACLEA, 2007).

Universities that operate off-campus locations or satellite campuses face a special challenge in emergency planning. Branch campuses, as they are sometimes called, tend not to have the presence of emergency response personnel associated with the main campus; in fact, it is not uncommon for security to be provided through contract arrangements. More importantly, off-campus locations tend to receive emergency police, fire, and medical services from jurisdictions other than those that respond to incidents on the main campus. These factors increase the complexity of the emergency planning process but certainly do not present irresolvable challenges. A standard practice is to establish interagency agreements, commonly referred to as *mutual aid agreements*, that allow sharing personnel, equipment, and logistical and procedural resources across jurisdictional boundaries (IACLEA, 2007). Emergency planning for branch campuses can and should use the same basic structures as those used on the main campus; that is, emergency plans for such locations should be NIMS-compliant EOPs that incorporate the Incident Command System. Training of personnel at off-campus locations for emergency response is especially important because the geographic separation suggests that at least initially incidents at such locations will have to be managed without the support of the resources of the main campus. Institutional leaders should be mindful that the provisions of the federal Higher Education Opportunity Act (2008), mandating disclosure of agreements with outside emergency response agencies, emergency response and evacuation procedures, missing person procedures, and annual testing of emergency response procedures, apply to all academic delivery sites.

Regardless of whether an institution is a single-campus or multi-campus organization, the NIMS advises certain assumptions for emergency response planning. Key among these assumptions is that in large-scale disasters or crises, institutions should plan to be self-sufficient for at least the initial response phase and perhaps longer (IACLEA, 2007). The reason for this assumption is that in large-scale events cooperating agencies that have mutual aid agreements may find themselves obligated to respond in their own jurisdictions and not be available for response or recovery operations and support. Such an assumption has a fundamental impact on the approach an institution will take in planning when personnel and supplies may be scarce or unavailable, and cooperating agencies are unable to assist. The creative and intentional use of campus resources is critical during large-scale disasters, and student affairs professionals can provide leadership related to the facilitation of basic-need resources during such crises. Specifically, a CRT can serve a key function in the self-sufficient response of an institution.

Student Affairs CRTs

Much like the ICP and IC, another tactical function will be met by the institution's student affairs staff (or similar designee). For the purpose of this chapter, this critical function will be referred to as a CRT, although the scope of response may extend beyond NIMS-defined crises (U.S. Department of Homeland Security, Federal Bureau of Investigation, & International Association of Campus Law Enforcement Administrators, 2006). As the EOC personnel provide strategic oversight of the emergency situation and the ICP/IC provides on-site management and response, the CRT is a third body that can manage the individualized response to the crisis and act on the strategic decisions made by the executive leadership team of the university. But what does a CRT look like, and how does this group distinguish itself from the EOC and ICP/IC?

There is a distinct difference between simply having a solid conceptual model or plan for crisis response and having an active CRT. The reality is that *your campus needs both*. Every student affairs division ideally has a comprehensive crisis response plan that aligns with the overarching EOP for its campus. In addition to this, it is critical to take this plan one step further: A student affairs CRT should be actively meeting (e.g., weekly, biweekly, or monthly) and addressing all levels of student crises and concerns, whether these require EOC activation or not. Although this is an important step, June (2007) found that "71% of [survey] respondents said that the crisis teams at their institutions did not meet on a regular basis" (p. 7).

The purpose of a CRT is to provide a response mechanism that is broad and comprehensive in its approach during each student-related crisis. While some campuses like to centralize such an operation and give the responsibility for crisis response to Residential Life or Judicial Affairs, it can be argued that these units have a narrow scope of operation and rarely have much influence beyond the parameters of their daily work. This limited scope and empowerment can hinder their approach to crisis response. Placing the responsibility for active crisis response in the office of the senior student affairs officer (SSAO) provides a better opportunity for the employment of a comprehensive, team-based approach. A cross-functional team promotes better analysis of the crisis at hand and ultimately provides for a more thorough response and support to the student. The purview of the office of the SSAO allows for more timely and complete access to information, resources, and support in a time of crisis.

Such a team should be appointed by the SSAO and should consider individuals' roles within the organization, not an individual's interest in crisis management. Individuals on this team should have sufficient responsibility and authority in their roles on campus to effectively and efficiently exercise the tactical needs of the campus during a crisis. Most importantly, decision makers need to be on the CRT. If the team is made up of great minds with no authority to make decisions, valuable time and institutional credibility could be lost in a crisis. The team must be cross-functional and represent the multifaceted aspects of students on campus (e.g., where they live, how they are involved, how they culturally/socially identify, etc.). It is important to note that the individual who chairs this team should *not* be the SSAO. Although this seems counterintuitive, the reality is that in a major crisis or disaster situation such as an active shooter the SSAO will be required to provide leadership for the campus EOP. The SSAO will likely serve a predesignated role as a member of the campus EOC staff requiring him or her to actively address broader institutional response and direction. Thus, the chair of the CRT should be the most capable leader one level below the SSAO (e.g., associate or assistant vice president/chancellor/dean). This individual must be highly capable and empowered to make important decisions in the absence of the SSAO.

Each campus may approach CRT composition in a different way, but key individuals should be engaged. These include the SSAO (ex-officio), leaders who report directly to the SSAO and who can act in his or her absence (e.g., associate/assistant vice presidents), the director of counseling, the director of student health, the director(s) of housing (both on- and off-campus housing), public relations liaison, key diversity officers, and director of student activities. To establish a solid CRT, the SSAO must consider the most prevalent aspects of student life and appoint related staff. For instance, if the campus has a large commuter population, it would be critical to include a staff member responsible for commuter services. It is also important that this team have the ability to tap into the assistance of other areas on an ad hoc basis. For instance, in the event of a sexual assault, a director of women's resources or director of wellness might be the logical professional to bring to the table (even if the person is not a CRT member).

Each CRT should receive a comprehensive procedure manual, and the chair should reserve time annually to review the contents and make additions and updates. The procedure manual should include information for student affairs personnel on topics such as

- purpose and philosophy of the team
- general protocol for responding to student crises in specific areas (e.g., residence hall, Greek housing, nonresidential facility, study abroad)
- specific protocol when dealing with a student death
- procedures related to addressing specified events involving but not limited to sexual assault, active shooter, and family crisis
- protocols related to interacting with media
- protocols related to campus infrastructure needs during crises (e.g., housing, dining, health center, recreation services, transportation, etc.)

Beyond the manual, impromptu tabletop exercises should be conducted annually to keep skills and thoughtful processing a fresh part of the team's skill set (Carey, 2006); ideally, training of this nature could align with the EOP-related exercises. Realistically, the most effective training of these teams is often on the job. The more frequently the team meets and addresses crises (acute or otherwise), the more efficient and effective it will become. Tabletop or staged training has the potential to become secondary as the team meets frequently to address student and family crises, ingraining the work of crisis response in the culture of student affairs. Additionally, training and protocols are often an organic evolution of the team's interactions and length of time the members work together.

Ideally, the CRT becomes the tactical or actively functioning extension of the campus EOP. Allowing for frequent and supportive crisis intervention on behalf of the institution, without employing the resources and effort involved with the full emergency management plan, is a more efficient crisis management model.

The CRT should maintain at least five formal connections/relationships to be most successful. These include collaborative relationships with the local hospital(s), campus/local police, the public relations staff, campus legal counsel, and the office of the president (or the designated emergency management liaison). These direct relationships should be actively cultivated by those on the CRT to be most effective and efficient in a crisis.

CRTs will often deal with acute crises that require immediate assistance and follow-through. For instance, in the event of a student death because of an automobile accident, an active CRT would be notified of the accident and immediately meet to assess the situation and create a plan of action. A typical agenda for such a situation would include the following:

1. Share all facts related to the student crisis.
2. Share what is known about the student and the student's engagement with the campus (e.g., academic records, housing records, judicial records, student organization involvement/ records, Internet social groups).
3. Identify immediate action items and discuss tactical decisions (e.g., connect with the hospital to obtain information, connect with police to obtain information, identify for the family the victim liaison [discussed in the next section] who will make official contact on behalf of the college, contact the academic office to make the death notification, reach out to faculty personally to

inform them of the death, initiate the appropriate paperwork to freeze student records and avoid unnecessary mailings to the family).
4. Identify additional action items (e.g., Are there any communities of concern? Are counselors needed? What will be the ripple effects in the community? Does the team need to work with a residential community or assist with removing personal effects from an off-campus apartment? What else should the team do?).

The more active the CRT becomes, the more conditioned the members become in bringing relevant data to the table and in responding more quickly and thoroughly to the situation. Additionally, the more conditioned the team is the more adept it will be in responding to a major campus crisis such as an active shooter. Simply put, much of crisis response is learned behavior that can be developed in the staff well before the time of need (Carey, 2006; Jablonski, McClellan, & Zdziarski, 2008).

Victim Liaisons

Providing victim liaisons can be an effective crisis response tactic (Jablonski, McClellan, & Zdziarski, 2008). This service can be provided by student affairs professionals and developed as an extension of the CRT. The role of the victim liaison is to provide immediate, individualized, accurate, and sustained support to the designated victims of the crisis. Ideally, an institution would organize and train multiple individuals to serve as victim liaisons on a victim liaison team that would be activated in totality or individually as the crisis dictated.

Various definitions are used to describe a victim of a crime, particularly during a campus shooting. For instance, primary victims may be classified as individuals who are physically injured or killed during the incident. Secondary victims could be individuals at the scene of the incident, such as witnesses who were not physically injured. Family members, significant others, or close friends of the primary victims who suffer mentally and physically because of the incident would be categorized as secondary victims. Employees of the institution would be affected by the incident to varying degrees, but generally not to the level of a primary or secondary victim. In developing immediate response procedures for a campus shooting, the institution should articulate the definition of victim that will be used to establish and mobilize a victim liaison team.

Victim liaison teams are composed of university employees who serve as agents of the institution, and as such the scope of their options for responding to victims' needs will be defined by university authorization and resources. While the liaison may provide information about nonuniversity resources (e.g., state crime victim compensation programs) and assist with completing related applications if requested by the victim, the liaison role does not encompass the broad range of supportive services that state-appointed victim advocates are typically trained to provide (for example, see http://www.illi noisattorneygeneral.gov/victims/index.html). Liaisons are principally charged with identifying and helping to address victims' current needs, facilitating victims' access to university and selected external resources, helping victims navigate university procedures involving their academic status and financial aid, serving as the primary communication channel between the university and the affected students and families, and helping to protect victims' privacy in the wake of a very public incident.

In recruiting liaisons from the current professional staff, certain individual characteristics can be pivotal in the creation and maintenance of a viable victim liaison team. These include but are not limited to the following:

- strong communication skills
- interpersonal skills, ability to establish relationships of trust
- professionalism including integrity, reliability, adaptability, accuracy
- personal characteristics including sensitivity, stamina, emotional strength, maturity
- dedication to students, experience working with students
- bilingual language skills relevant to the campus community
- commitment to fulfilling the liaison role in an objective yet compassionate manner.

The liaison role is likely to be exceedingly time consuming. Depending on the crisis, the liaison may not be able to resume normal duties for some time and may thus need to be released temporarily from work responsibilities to accommodate liaison activities.

Beyond recruitment, the uniqueness of each incident will require that victim liaisons receive adequate training for addressing a multitude of situational conditions and needs. While one can never fully prepare for every crisis, essential training for victim liaisons should include but would not be limited to the following:

> ➤ the role of the liaison (i.e., authority, scope of activity) as an agent of the university at funerals, memorial services, hospital visits, and so on
> ➤ legal considerations pertaining to campus injuries and deaths (e.g., liability, university response measures, available university resources)
> ➤ emotional reactions of trauma victims and appropriate support techniques
> ➤ expectations for communicating with victims/family members, campus entities, external agencies
> ➤ confidentiality of privileged victim/family information (e.g., medical condition and treatment plans, financial circumstances, academic and financial aid status)
> ➤ protection of victim/family privacy (e.g., deflecting undesired contacts and solicitations, understanding the limitations of the Family Educational Rights and Privacy Act (FERPA, 2008) and the Health Insurance Portability and Accountability Act (HIPAA, 1996)
> ➤ university operations, campus services and procedures (e.g., academic withdrawals, financial aid procedures, university refunds) outside the liaison's usual scope of activity
> ➤ liaison self-care and support during highly emotional and challenging service of uncertain duration

A liaison coordinator function, ideally a member of the CRT, is critical to the maintenance of a well-trained and optimally functioning team of liaisons. In addition to recruiting and ensuring appropriate training for the team, the coordinator serves as an ongoing resource and guide for active liaisons. By providing a facilitative function between university officials (e.g., student affairs, legal services, academic deans, registrar) and the liaison team, the coordinator serves as a communication clearinghouse in providing liaisons with consistent, relevant, and timely information; assists with liaison problem solving; oversees liaison activity with regard to institutional expectations and parameters; and monitors the emotional status of liaisons, making referrals or arranging for timely support at the liaison's request. If applicable, the coordinator assists with the transition of the liaison function from team members to the dedicated university department or unit that will provide long-term support for all victims until their graduation or separation from the institution. Although the timing of this transition would depend on the nature and magnitude of the incident and the university's ability to establish a permanent office to provide support, the liaison function would ideally be concluded within 4 to 6 weeks of the incident.

Coordination of Resources

Planning for crises dictates that myriad resources available to institutions and victims be understood prior to the occurrence of an incident; their appropriate coordination and interplay is also paramount. It is essential for campus leaders and victim liaisons to maintain current information about federal, state, and local resources that could provide assistance and best serve victims. For example, knowledge of eligibility criteria, application processes, deadlines, and maximum program benefits of such services could prove invaluable when offering assistance to a victim via a victim liaison program or otherwise.

Federal, State, and Local Resources

Institutional leaders should become familiar with federal and state emergency management agencies, as they are critical partners in the event of a crisis, and governors have the authority to declare an emergency and subsequently request federal assistance (Federal Emergency Management Agency [FEMA], 2007). In addition, entities such as the Department of Justice, Department of Education, Department of Homeland Security, American Red Cross, and Salvation Army offer grants or other assistance to cover emergency response expenses. Depending on state and federal statutes, there may be reimbursement for specific expenses to assist crime victims. Having an understanding of these various benefits and procedures can facilitate a more effective campus response to crisis.

As mentioned earlier, a NIMS-compliant campus EOP will provide coordinated local resources. If a campus does not have such a plan, it is essential that formal protocols for responding to a crisis be developed prior to any incident, especially with external entities such as local law enforcement agencies and fire and emergency medical personnel. With such plans, local health care personnel, especially first responders, would triage to treat victims on site and transfer others to facilities better equipped to handle various types of trauma. Campuses can work with the local police and fire networks to provide crime scene assistance. The involvement of these networks will be vital in an emergency medical and mutual aid response; this includes transportation of injured and deceased victims.

Campus- and Community-Based Resources

Once an incident is reported and the EOP activated, it is imperative that resources from several internal constituents be available immediately. For instance, campus police would be critical in an emergency response, especially if the shooter is still active. The police would establish crime scene jurisdiction and assist medical personnel with setting up a triage area to assist victims. Other campus units may be able to provide resources including limited medical care offered through health services, campus ministry to address spiritual needs, and the counseling center to offer trauma counseling in collaboration with faculty who possess expertise in trauma counseling. Many of these resources or services would be deployed by the CRT, which would gather at the earliest notification of a crisis and begin to authorize and coordinate resources.

While organizing and providing information and offering assistance to students and families will be essential, other campus entities will be integral to the crisis response. Specifically, the employee assistance/counseling program could serve as a resource for faculty and staff affected by the trauma, while information technology (IT) staff could assist with communication needs through the Internet or telephone lines. In addition, public affairs would be responsible for holding press conferences (with assistance from IT) as well as facilitating media access and the presence of media on campus.

After the immediate needs of the primary and secondary victims have been met on the day of the incident, additional resources will be needed. For instance, countywide mental health agencies would need to be prepared for the increased demand from established clients as well as for referrals from the institution to assist with the overload that campus counselors would be experiencing. Moreover, state mental health services could offer counseling assistance, which would be coordinated by the campus or through a state agency (Kennedy, 2008). The benefits, procedures, and timelines of such programs would need to be clearly delineated for the victim. Thus, it is important that the victim liaison coordinator maintain current information and related procedures for all resources to ensure that the information is accurate and clearly communicated during a crisis.

Unfortunately, a pronouncement of death will be required for any mortally wounded victims. Subsequently, the coroner's office would collect medical and forensic evidence for the deceased, issue the death notification, and may offer family assistance. Contrary to common perceptions, campus or local police agencies do not address this situation but take guidance from the coroner (Blakeney, 2002). When the coroner's work is complete, the body would be released to a licensed funeral director of the family's choice.

Additional Considerations

Every campus shooting will present its own set of challenges requiring the institution to be flexible in its predetermined EOP. In preparation, institutional leadership should attempt to determine what expenses might be covered because of a campus shooting or large-scale crisis. The details should be considered in advance rather than

during the incident when emotions are unpredictable. These decisions may be dictated or influenced by a number of considerations,
for instance: What is included in the campus insurance policy? Is the
institution religiously affiliated? Are there unique campus partners
that could aid in the response? Campus leaders should clarify the
timing of the support offered, such as if the institution will be the
primary or last payer. Such financial support could include medical
expenses; destroyed or lost items not returned to students such as
backpacks, cellular telephones, laptops, clothing, and textbooks;
funeral expenses; family travel expenses for funerals and memorial
services; and housing and other support for volunteer professionals
who assist during the early recovery phase and at subsequent remembrance events.

To determine the costs of a shooting-related incident, the immediate and long-term expenses (ranging from the initial costs to the long-
term recovery costs) must be considered. Beyond the expenses
related to the immediate crisis response, there would be costs for
events and ceremonies (see chapter 6) related to the incident in the
form of facilities, audiovisual services, printing costs, flowers, staffing
to support campus activities, and other expenditures specific to an
institution or activity. Possibly there might be an increased demand
and referrals for counseling services that could be manifested
through the increased work hours of staff in those areas. The number
of requests for assistance from counselors, faculty, and administration might soar because of the perception of unpredictable or odd
student behaviors, thereby creating another cost to be borne by the
institution. Depending on the nature of the incident and the availability of campus resources, there could be ongoing, long-term costs
for specific support of victims' needs.

Monetary contributions will be made to the institution, as well as
donations of goods and services, which will require a committee or
designees to discern appropriate uses for these resources. For example, monetary donations could be used to establish a scholarship program in memory of the victims or to assist those who were injured in
the shooting. Goods and services such as food, memorial ribbons,
air travel, or other items could be useful when planning memorial
services.

The institution-wide and student health insurance policy should be analyzed annually. The maximum benefit should be reviewed and adjusted as needed to address anticipated medical expenses for a victim of a campus shooting so that out-of-pocket costs a victim would have to pay would be minimal. In reviewing the policy, ensure that victim injuries that occur as a result of crimes or acts of violence are not excluded. Most importantly, the plan should include a death benefit. Relative to the insurance policy for the institution, there should be insurance benefits for deceased students. Moreover, benefits for ongoing health care costs, as well as for items destroyed or not returned after the incident, should be included in the institutional policy.

Threat Assessment Teams

Given the incidents of unexpected school and campus violence that have captured the nation's attention in recent years, the concept of a proactive threat assessment process to prevent targeted campus violence has been gaining momentum. Although there is no way to anticipate random violence such as a campus shooter, a campus threat assessment team (TAT) can be appointed to assess known threats and if necessary take early action and diffuse potentially violent situations. Indeed, following the shootings at Virginia Tech and Northern Illinois University, Virginia and Illinois enacted legislation requiring the establishment of TATs on university campuses (Deisenger, Randazzo, O'Neill, & Savage, 2008).

"A Threat Assessment and Management Team is a multidisciplinary team that is responsible for the careful and contextual identification and evaluation of behaviors that raise concern and that may precede violent activity on campus" (Deisenger et al., 2008, p. 5). A TAT evaluates the risk of targeted violence to the campus community and makes a recommendation to administration regarding appropriate intervention(s) and follow-up in a given case. When establishing a TAT, it is important for the institution to consider the role and composition of the team and the training it will receive. It is important that the team be able to act in a timely manner to review all reported information, seek additional details as needed, and communicate recommendations for relevant interventions, as well as to ensure that sufficient follow-up is conducted postintervention. It is also important that the TAT have a sufficient range of options (e.g., involuntary withdrawal policy) at its disposal for determining a best course of action in a given situation (Working Group, 2007). The TAT is not, however, an emergency response entity; the institution's established emergency response procedures should be activated in the event of a true campus emergency.

If not mandated by state statute, the TAT membership, scope of authority, and procedures are determined by the institution. Members would reasonably include administrators from student affairs (e.g., associate and assistant vice presidents; directors of health and counseling services and housing and dining), enrollment services, legal services, university police, and other areas with responsibility for campus safety (Working Group, 2007). Selection of the team chair would reflect the appropriate organizational line of authority. Membership crossover between a campus TAT and CRT should be considered advantageous.

A TAT must have adequate training about the threat assessment process to fulfill its role on campus (see for example, the Campus Security Enhancement Act, 2008). Training may be achieved through required readings, conference attendance, and expert training on the threat assessment process; exercises and drills also provide valuable reinforcement of threat assessment principles, strategies, and procedures for team members.

Since the TAT will receive, analyze, and act on information from a variety of sources, training must also address the legal requirements applicable to retention, security, and release of student information. Appropriate procedures must be developed and maintained in consultation with the institution's legal counsel and additional administrative areas as needed (e.g., IT, registration, campus police, counseling, medical, financial aid, etc.), and team members must be familiar with the restrictions as well as the opportunities pertaining to information management at any given time. For example, FERPA (2008) permits disclosure of "personally identifiable information from an education record to appropriate parties, including parents of eligible student, in connection with an emergency if knowledge of the information is necessary to protect the health and safety of the student or other individuals" (§ 99.36). At the same time, FERPA-exempt health records may be subject to HIPAA (1996) and/or state confidentiality requirements, underscoring the need for clarity and accuracy in operating procedures and training for TAT members.

In addition to training implications, information management for a TAT must address the mechanics of recordkeeping (e.g., data collection, processing, storage, retrieval, retention, and disposal), the nature and potential requirements pertaining to records generated by the team (e.g., education records subject to FERPA [2008], discoverability), and potential student rights (i.e., whether a student must be informed of the presence of a TAT record). Institutional legal counsel is an essential member in these discussions and procedural decisions.

While the TAT will fulfill a critical role in the broad scope of maintaining campus safety, team function will require a significant allocation of resources in the form of time, training, and staffing. The time required to attend anticipated weekly meetings for a potentially large group of members would be one resource to consider. Training is another resource the institution would need, as speakers or consultants, conference attendance (including related travel costs), and reference materials would be necessary.

Communication During Crises

The single most important element in an effective crisis response is efficient communication (Nash, 2007). This includes communication among responders, communication with key constituents and communities, as well as communication with the media. The simple task of communicating during a crisis can be quite challenging; therefore, it is important to be thoughtful and highly detailed when planning for communication during a crisis. Although an NIMS-compliant EOP addresses a wide range of response functions, communications during a large-scale emergency or crisis situation is of special importance. Emergency communication is often thought of in terms of print and electronic media. However, when engaged in

NIMS-compliant emergency response planning, communications during crisis conditions take on multiple aspects—some focused on incident command, some focused on warning and alert, and some related to traditional media relations. Communications plans will span the longevity of the crisis, from warning to update to recovery phases of emergency operations.

Emergency Notification

Institutions' administrators must think broadly about the media to be used for emergency notification and warning. Incidents such as September 11, and those at Virginia Tech and Northern Illinois University, have illustrated the vulnerability of standard communications media, including cell phones and Web postings. Officials are well advised to think of a range of warning systems, from low tech (e.g., sirens, lights, loudspeakers) to high tech (e.g., cell phones, text messaging, mass e-mail) that are redundant. This issue is addressed in the federal Higher Education Opportunity Act (2008) that mandates institutions to annually notify campus constituents of emergency response and evacuation procedures, including use of electronic communication systems (§ 488e; Selingo, 2008).

Campus Responders

The technology that supports communication has a profound effect on staff members' ability to connect to one another on campus and to reach others off campus. Adopting redundant communication features for campus responders is also highly encouraged. Communication tools are numerous: They include landline phones, cell phones, voice mail, Web sites, e-mail, text messaging, instant messaging, and others. Of these, phones are the most commonplace tool used in crisis response situations. In that vein, there is a clear trend requesting or requiring campuses to purchase emergency text messaging systems (Jablonski et al., 2008; Selingo, 2008).

During the Northern Illinois University shooting, students, faculty, and staff found using cell phones (making calls and text messaging) to be unreliable and at times service was not available. Some campuses maintain corporate accounts with specific cell phone companies, and the tendency is to rely on this form of communication in times of crisis. When this is the case, use of that one carrier may exceed the typical ability to support those cell phone accounts. Additionally, cell phones and text messaging are not highly secure, and like most technologies they have limitations and vulnerabilities that are important to keep in mind (Bambenek & Klus, 2008; Galuszka, 2008). Campus leaders should not overlook the capabilities of landline phone systems and should work with their technology staff to fully understand the capabilities of landline phone systems and how to leverage those features during a crisis.

Students, faculty, and staff during the crisis at Northern Illinois University found that landline phones, instant messaging, and the campus Web site were the most helpful and productive means of communicating internally and externally. Campuses should be encouraged to maintain an internal instant message system, as it would become invaluable during a large-scale crisis when cell phones prove unreliable. Additionally, CRT members should possess handheld or two-way radios to communicate with one another during the immediate crisis. In the event of an active shooter, members of the campus community will be scattered and some will be in hiding until they feel safe; having alternative and low-tech communication systems is critical to keep the response effort moving forward in the midst of chaos. The campus Web site is an amazing tool for communicating externally. Frequent updates and streaming information can be used to convey information and updates quickly to students, faculty, staff, families, and media, among others.

In relation to campus communication, it is important to highlight two specific campus communities. It is imperative that student affairs address the specific communication challenges and needs of students with physical disabilities or impairments, as well as students or families with limited English language skills. Select campus notification systems or evacuation procedures may need to be tailored to meet the needs of these students. All members of the campus community will feel they are at a disadvantage during a major campus crisis, but these individuals have important needs and situations that must be considered and planned for in advance.

Media Relations

Working effectively with the media is another critical aspect of communication during a crisis. In a large-scale incident, the institution's EOP will define the person and office on campus responsible for communication with the media. Typically, this will be the public relations office. If a campus does not have a public relations staff, one must be identified for the purposes of crisis response (Nash, 2007). Having a centralized media contact is nonnegotiable and hazardous to disregard. It is critical that the messages related to the campus crisis be credible, consistent, and coordinated, and this is best done by designating one centralized office to lead this effort. Communicating messages in this manner will minimize the public perception that the organization is unable to handle the situation appropriately (Nash).

Assuming there is a campus public relations office, it is critical for student affairs to have a preestablished public relations liaison serving on, or working with, the CRT. If the public relations liaison is a preestablished and actively operating position, there will be less confusion during a time of crisis. With this position in place, student affairs staff will more naturally turn to that individual for leadership related to media instead of speaking to media directly. The student affairs public relations liaison will feed media requests to the centralized public relations office and guide the CRT on any media-related instructions.

During a major campus crisis, such as an active shooter, it can be expected that media will converge on campus looking for more information and firsthand accounts of the incident. It is important that campus leaders approach these relationships looking for a win-win scenario. The media outlets will rely on the campus to provide information and access to individuals for interviews, but in turn, campus officials can ask media partners to assist them in the crisis management and prioritize the messages that get sent to the general public. The initial and most critical messages are the status updates regarding the situation at hand. Once the situation is under control, the next wave of critical information is to provide families and community members with a way to connect to the campus and ask questions (e.g., hotlines or support services).

If the campus is located in close proximity to a large metropolitan area, or if the incident is of extraordinary newsworthiness, there is a good chance that media vans and crews will rapidly proliferate. Campuses should decide in advance how they plan to communicate with these crews and how they will support them (e.g., meeting technological requests, shelter in severe weather, and food needs). Campuses should be equally alert to the need for training and simulation for media relations under emergency conditions (Nash, 2008). Training should address dealing with media, both friendly and hostile, during single-event incidents as well as sustained crises.

Press conferences are a good avenue to provide the known details of the crisis to many reporters at once. In fact, offering multiple press conferences (reasonably spaced throughout the day) during a major campus crisis can alleviate the pressures of the media. Of course, press conferences require facilities, specific technologies, and resources. Having highly detailed and flexible plans in place is critical to effective crisis response.

Public relations staff will look to student affairs staff for many media-related requests. For instance, there will be requests to speak with students or certain staff members critical to the crisis response (e.g., counselors), and there may be requests for bilingual staff to speak on behalf of the institution. The CRT must be prepared for these types of requests and consider how to respond. Again, the student affairs public relations liaison can help manage these requests and expectations. With the right relationships in place and the appropriate leadership and authority, this CRT member can leverage his or her contact with media to get critical information out to the public while providing access to relevant and competent content experts who can represent the institution to the media.

Crisis Hotlines

Another avenue of communication during crisis conditions that should not be overlooked is the crisis hotline, because one of the more challenging issues is responding to the general public's need for information. The Web site can convey critical information and help to quickly spread updates regarding the situation, but a parent who is located two states away and needs information about his or her child is something entirely different (Merriman, 2008). Many people will want to speak directly to someone with information. The need to provide accurate, timely, and reliable information to campus constituents about current and emerging conditions cannot be understated. During large-scale incidents, campus constituents will seek information on assembly points, safe havens, means for communicating with external parties (e.g., parents of students, families of employees), and advisories on safety conditions on campus.

There will eventually be a need to communicate information related to institutional recovery. Crisis situations may lead to a prolonged campus closure. When that occurs, many questions arise about course completion, extension of the academic term, change in examination schedules and commencement dates, postevent performance expectations for students and faculty, and other operational questions. Although these may seem like unimportant details given the greater context of the crisis, these issues take on proportions far beyond the mundane for the student who is graduating and is committed to a firm start date in employment or internship, for the family that has incurred major financial expenses for travel arrangements to a commencement, for traumatized students and employees who need support upon resumption of institutional operations, and for the faculty members who experience disruption and the same psychological trauma as other campus constituents. The quality of institutional communication related to recovery issues provides the campus community with a sense of certainty, control, and normality, and it speeds resumption of campus operations. The communication strategies planned for and used by the institution during the recovery phase of crisis management should account for these considerations, which are often overlooked.

Crisis hotlines are a necessary aspect of any crisis plan and an effective way to offer the general public a direct connection to internal institutional representatives. During the Northern Illinois University shooting, crisis hotlines were established and the numbers posted on the Web site within 45 minutes of the incident's report. These lines, seven in total, were staffed 24 hours a day for 4 days and 12 hours a day for the following 10 days. These seven phone lines handled 19,000 calls, over 15,000 of which came within the first 24 hours.

In the operation of a crisis hotline, numerous issues must be considered. To begin with, where will it be housed? Many campuses have annual fund-raising call centers or similar rooms that are a great option for this type of crisis response mechanism. An important thing to keep in mind is the proximity of the hotline operation to the EOC or CRT, where information is streaming to during the crisis. In order to provide timely updates to the staff taking calls, these operational centers should be relatively close to one another. Administrators of some campuses may shy away from establishing such an operation for fear they will not have details to share with the general public. The reality is that having operators with little information but offering support and directions on how to obtain updates will serve the institution far better than not offering this assistance.

Another question might be: Who should staff these phone lines? Campus officials must be thoughtful about those who are tapped to staff the phones. Administrators should be sure these individuals are identified in advance (via the crisis plan), and they should seek individuals with counseling or advising experience, as the skill sets they possess will be helpful to anxious and traumatized callers (Merriman, 2008). Recruiting bilingual staff to respond to calls from non-English-speaking individuals and consulates should also be considered. All these individuals should be fully trained and clearly understand their role and how it interplays with FERPA (2008) and other institutional policies regarding student files and communication with nonstudents during a crisis.

Information Management During Crises

To this point, basic communication has been addressed, but the responsibility extends beyond communication and is a task of information management. What is done with the information, and how it is secured, is as critical as attaining it through established relationships. A CRT will communicate with a number of constituents: the EOC, hospital personnel, police, students, and the general public.

Interactions with each of these groups must be carefully considered and planned for in advance. Much of this relates to the previously mentioned relationships that must be established and maintained by the CRT.

What type of information will be helpful for crisis response? Hospital staff have a client/patient relationship with strict expectations of confidentiality (e.g., HIPAA [1996]). Yet, if relationships have been built in advance with local hospital administration and staff, these individuals are more likely to welcome campus assistance in a crisis, and this collaborative tone will help the EOC and CRT serve victims and students in a more effective and efficient way. For instance, by simply being in the hospital waiting room with students and families, student affairs staff are able to hear the initial wishes and needs of their students. With this direct connection, student affairs and the larger campus community can put their resources to work to best serve the students and families in need. Connected to this notion, preestablished relationships and understandings with police (on and off campus) can serve a similar purpose. The police can provide the CRT with current data related to victims and students in need in a timely fashion.

The accumulated information from the hospital and the police can be easily summarized and augmented by judicial files, student activities files, threat assessment information, as well as Internet social networking information, to create a helpful portfolio on every student directly involved with the crisis. When information is pooled in such a manner, the EOC and CRT can more easily relate to the students in need, and gain a broader understanding of the impact of the situation as it relates to the campus community. For instance, if a student who has been killed was an active member of a student organization, related counseling support and other resources can be deployed effectively and directly.

Being more proactive rather than waiting for a student group to request support has long-term implications in working with your campus community. Expedient information management related to crisis can assist with operational details performed by the institution that will create goodwill. For example, officials at the institution would not want the bursar to send bills to victims, nor would campus leaders want victims' cars ticketed or towed. In a crisis scenario, every institutional action must be scrutinized through a lens of sensitivity. These simple details can determine how the institution will be perceived by the general public. To that end, the value of early and accurate collection, pooling, and appropriate dissemination of information can never be understated.

At some point after the initial crisis (ideally within the next 24 to 36 hours), outreach should take place in a thoughtful and organized manner with the direct victims. This outreach should be made by a separate and smaller group of callers and should include victim liaisons. In the case of a classroom shooting, the priority population for these calls should include the families of the deceased students; physically injured students; students enrolled in the classroom (whether they were in attendance or not); any witnesses faculty or staff are aware of through personal accounts, photographs, or police documentation; and the family of the perpetrator (if appropriate). The outreach effort should focus on connecting these students and families to counseling resources, assisting with enrollment/academic concerns, addressing collection of personal items left at the scene of the incident, and assessing any additional needs. These types of calls should continue in a frequent (e.g., weekly or more often) fashion for some period of time postincident as a means of continually monitoring students' reactions and trauma. All of these calls should be documented and appropriate referrals made, with follow-up as necessary.

Conclusion

Violence on campus, given the storied culture and traditions of the American academy, is likely to be a turning point in the life of the institution. Random and senseless violence has the potential to fundamentally alter the character and operations of a campus. While an institution cannot fully prepare for a crisis, developing a thorough EOP coupled with thoughtful services and communication can facilitate an effective response to an emergency situation. Most importantly, student affairs professionals maintain an integral role in campus crisis response and facilitate critical services. A carefully constructed emergency plan, augmented by a CRT and victim liaisons and executed by well-trained and practiced professionals, is the best architecture for responding to a campus in crisis.

References

Bambenek, J., & Klus, A. (2008). Do emergency text messaging systems put students in more danger? *Education Quarterly*, 3, 12–15.

Blakeney, R. L. (2002). *Providing relief to families after a mass fatality: Roles of the medical examiner's office and the family assistance center.* Retrieved from http://www.ojp.usdoj.gov/ovc/publications/bulletins/prfmf_11_2001/188912.pdf

Campus Security Enhancement Act of 2008, 110 ILCS 12. Retrieved from http://www.ilga.gov/legislation/ilcs/ilcs3.asp?ActID=1054&ChapAct=110%26nbsp%3BILCS%26nbsp%3B12%2F&ChapterID=18&ChapterName=HIGHER+EDUCATION&ActName=Campus+Security+Enhancement+Act+of+2008

Carey, R. (2006). The art of anticipation: You can't predict a campus crisis, but you can prepare for what you should do if one happens on your watch. *Chronicle of Higher Education*, 52(45), C1.

Deisinger, G., Randazzo, M., O'Neill, D., & Savage, J. (2008). *The handbook for campus threat assessment & management teams.* Stoneham, MA: Applied Risk Management.

Family Educational Rights and Privacy Act, 2008.

Family Educational Rights and Privacy: Final Rule. Federal Register, Part II: Department of Education, §34 CFR Part 99, v73 n237 (December 9, 2008).

Federal Emergency Management Agency. (2007). *Public assistance guide.* Retrieved from http://www.fema.gov/pdf/government/grant/pa/pagdoc.pdf

Galuszka, P. (2008). Emergency notification in an instant. *Diverse: Issues High Education*, 25(2), 14–17.

Health Insurance Portability and Accountability Act of 1996, Pub. L. 104–191, 119 Stat. 1936.

Higher Education Opportunity Act of 2008, Pub. L. No. 110–315, 122 Stat. 3078 (2008).

International Association of Campus Law Enforcement Administrators. (2007). *Campus emergency operations planning guide.* West Hartford, CT: Author.

Jablonski, M., McClellan, G., & Zdziarski, E. (Eds.). (2008). *In search of safer communities: Emerging practices for student affairs in addressing campus violence.* Washington, DC: Student Affairs Administrators in Higher Education. Retrieved March 27, 2009, from www.naspa.org/files/SaferComm.pdf

June, W. (2007). Crisis-management plans are untested, survey says. *Chronicle of Higher Education*, 54(8), 25.

Kennedy, M. (2008). Mind shifts. *American School & University*, 80(11), 16–22.

Merriman, L. (2008). Managing parent involvement during crisis. *New Directions for Student Services, 122,* 57–66.

Nash, B. F. (2007, Jul/Aug). Communications: The key to crisis response. *Campus Safety Magazine.*

Selingo, J. (2008). College leaders wrestle with how to prepare for unknown threats. *Chronicle of Higher Education, 54*(24), 17.

U.S. Department of Homeland Security. (2007). *National Incident Management System.* Retrieved from http://www.fema.gov/pdf/emergency/nims/NIMS_core.pdf

U.S. Department of Homeland Security, Federal Bureau of Investigation, & International Association of Campus Law Enforcement Administrators. (2006). *Campus public safety preparedness for catastrophic events: Lessons learned from hurricanes and explosives.* International Association of Campus Law Enforcement Administrators.

Working Group. (2007). *Presidential internal review: Working group report on the interface between Virginia Tech counseling services, academic affairs, judicial affairs and legal systems.* Retrieved June 12, 2009, from http://www.vtnews.vt.edu/documents/2007–08–22_internal_communications.pdf

4 Counseling During a Campus-Wide Crisis

Micky M. Sharma, Carolyn Bershad, and David LaBanc

THE ROLE of university counseling centers has transformed over the years and has been significantly affected by the mental health issues of each generation of college students, including the specific needs of the millennial generation (Howe & Strauss, 2003). More students with a past mental health history are going to college today, increasing the severity of mental health issues on campuses. In the 2008 National Survey of College Counseling Center Directors, 95% report that the trend of increasing numbers of students with severe psychological problems on campus remains true (Gallagher, 2008).

Attending college has become a viable option for students who may not have considered this a possibility in the 1980s, clearly a positive trend. However, this has changed the role of the counseling center director who spends an increasing amount of time in consultation with faculty, staff, and parents regarding "students of concern." Responding to mental health crises is a weekly, if not daily, responsibility. The director must be prepared to be consulted in the event of a large-scale campus crisis concerning the responses of the institution to mental health needs. This chapter outlines some specific guidelines for the mental health response to a campus shooting. Multiple key components are discussed, including the response to mental health needs, mobilization of resources, psychological first aid in classes, the psychological effects of trauma, and self-care. We assume the institution has a campus-based counseling center. For those colleges and universities without such a counseling center, decisions need to be made with respect to where mental health resources originate in the event of a crisis.

Immediate Response

The first step in determining how to respond during a crisis is to ensure that reports of a crisis are in fact accurate. Once information is verified, the counseling center staff should be briefed with all relevant facts. After this briefing, staff should be directed to take a moment to contact their loved ones to notify them of their safety and make necessary personal arrangements. Having staff do so at the beginning of a crisis will enable them to be more focused in their work.

The mental health response should be directed toward the location(s) of the primary and secondary victims (see pp. 62–67 in chapter 3). Clinicians should be deployed to multiple locations on campus where directly affected individuals are likely to be, while some staff should be kept at the center for students who walk in. Staff members at alternative locations should work in pairs if possible. Much of the initial clinical work across campus will be with groups, but some individuals may require one-on-one counseling. The area of the crisis is likely to be restricted; therefore, staff members should focus on residence halls, the student center or other gathering locations, and any student groups or departments immediately identified as being affected. Counselors meeting with individuals in remote locations must be focused on triage assessment and pay attention to those individuals in the most severe distress. Literature should be provided to individuals at all counseling locations so that victims may access services at a later date if needed. Finally, information about on-campus mental health resources and locations should be posted on the crisis response section of the university Web page.

The role of the counseling center's leadership will be pronounced. The director is likely to be out of the center for extended periods of times working with institutional administration. In his or her absence, a secondary leader should be predetermined to oversee the operations of the center and be involved in the staff deployment decisions. Effective and constant communication between the director and the leadership designee is paramount. The structure of this communication system should be in place in advance.

The immediate response may be more challenging for a counseling center composed of a single individual or a small staff. These centers should consider alternative on-campus faculty or staff members who could assist in the absence of typical counseling center leadership. While these individuals may not be mental health practitioners, they can provide leadership related to the response efforts.

Population Exposure Model

As planning is initiated to address campus mental health needs, it will be crucial to use a campus community perspective rather than one that focuses solely on the needs of discrete individuals. Multiple constituencies may require intervention beyond those directly affected by a traumatic event, and considering the collective needs of the campus community will be important as plans for intervention emerge.

A concentric circular Population Exposure Model can be helpful in this process to determine the various populations that may be affected by a campus trauma (Tucker, Pferrerbaum, Nixon, & Foy, 1999; U.S. Department of Health and Human Services [DHHS], 2004). The model's underlying principle is that the individuals who will be most greatly affected by a trauma are those who were most directly exposed to the trauma. One way to think of this is a ripple effect, referring to a stone thrown into a pond and the concentric rings of vibration from the stone that move outward through the water. Where the stone initially strikes is the area most affected, with the ripples becoming less intense as they move away from the center of impact.

Using this analogy, those individuals who were at the scene of the event, who witnessed the crisis, or who had loved ones or close friends at the crisis scene are typically the individuals who will be most affected by the event in question. This has been demonstrated in numerous studies (see, for example, Norris, Friedman, & Watson, 2002), and can provide a guide to managing resources and making decisions regarding intervention. However, it is important to remember that these kinds of generalizations do not always hold. There will often be individuals in various categories, even those relatively removed from the event, who are more vulnerable and may suffer a more severe reaction, and who may require more mental health intervention. Some may be at greater risk because of prior mental health problems, other life circumstances, or other risk factors.

Each campus community and each event will have its own set of affected populations. Figure 4.1 is one example of such a model.

A represents those individuals on campus most directly affected by the event, including their family members and close friends. B might include campus community members who were directly exposed to the incident and disaster scene but not injured. C could represent groups such as various bereaved extended family members, first responders, rescue workers, or service providers who were immediately involved with bereaved family members; who were immediately involved with individuals directly affected by the event; or who were obtaining information related to death notification or body identification. D might include mental health providers, clergy, chaplains,

Figure 4.1   Population Exposure Model

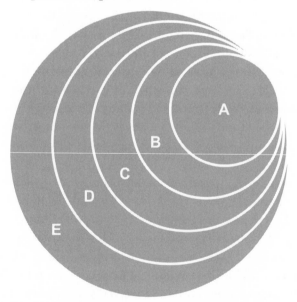

Note. From *Mental health response to mass violence and terrorism: A training manual*, by U.S. Department of Health and Human Services, DHHS Pub. No. SMA3959, 2004, Rockville, MD: Center for Mental Health Services, Substance Abuse and Mental Health Services Administration, p. 11.

emergency health care providers, and members of the media in general. E could include groups that might identify with the target-victim group or the larger surrounding community (Tucker et al., 1999; DHHS, 2004). Some individuals may belong to more than one category, so the model should serve as a heuristic, allowing for planning and response using a community perspective. Administrators should be aware of the various constituencies on their campuses and ascertain how they are interconnected as well as how they might work systematically with one another under traumatic circumstances. Over the course of each event, it will be important to ascertain who is directly and indirectly affected, as well as people's particular needs and how those needs might shift as time passes after the event.

Awareness of cultural and ethnic differences is paramount in this process so interventions may be planned that are culturally congruent and effective for each group. Bell (2008) notes how interventions that create social fabric, generate connectedness, help develop social skills, build self-esteem, and help minimize trauma can be retrofitted generally to be culturally sensitive with minimal effort. Bell purports that recognizing how a culture manifests these ideas and finding culturally congruent ways to express them will be important in working toward recovery. Bell gives the example of using a spirit quest exercise for Native Americans as a way to build esteem rather than building a sports team, which might be a more generic campus community approach. This consideration of culture means that mental health providers need to be aware not only of the campus culture at large but also of various constituencies and subcultures in the campus setting.

Immediate Psychological Responses to Trauma

Acute reactions among survivors immediately after a traumatic event can range from fright, panic, and hysteria to shock and numbness; reactions may be varied and can be quite intense. Most individuals who have survived a trauma will experience some sense of disbelief and disorientation, and some may even require medical attention for stress reactions. Others might want to help with rescue efforts, and emotional anguish and turmoil are not uncommon. Survivors can experience these various emotions simultaneously or sequentially, and emotions may shift over time. What is important to recognize is that each person's response will be specific to that person, and specific to the individual's experience of the trauma (DHHS, 2004).

Research has also shown that those who have more extreme and noticeable acute responses may be more likely to develop long-lasting and more severe post-trauma responses (Norris et al., 2002). Of the factors that influence the likelihood of long-standing or serious mental health problems, severity of exposure has been one of the strongest, defined by the number of stressors experienced, bereavement, injury to self or family, threat to life, or property or financial loss because of the event and subsequent relocation (Watson, 2008).

Reactions and expressions of grief may also need to be considered within each individual's social and cultural context. Thus, although someone's initial response may appear more extreme, it should also be evaluated with cultural sensitivity and the awareness that some groups are more expressive emotionally and use that emotional expressiveness to promote recovery through social connection. In addition, awareness of cultural traditions in mourning and healing should be encouraged for clinicians participating in support efforts to avoid stereotyping or *microaggressions* (Bell, 2008).

As with other mental health concerns, post-trauma reactions might be expressed through the various dimensions of human experience, including physical, behavioral, emotional, and cognitive. Common survivor reactions are listed in Figure 4.2 and can be used to help normalize a "normal reaction to an abnormal situation" (Flynn & Norwood, 2004; DHHS, 2004, pp. 16–17). These lists highlight that survivors' responses to trauma will be individualized and vary in intensity and range.

The breadth of these responses indicates that responders should not focus too much on one particular symptom, and that interventions should seek to address the needs of survivors across these various dimensions. Current literature suggests that people's reactions should not necessarily be regarded as pathological responses or even as precursors of a subsequent disorder; many people will have transient stress reactions in the aftermath of mass violence, and such

Figure 4.2   Common Trauma Survivor Reactions

Physical reactions may include
- Dizziness, faintness
- Hot/cold sensations in the body
- Agitation, nervousness, hyperarousal
- Appetite increase or decrease
- Headaches
- Tightness in throat, stomach, chest
- Shortness of breath
- Exacerbation of prior medical conditions

Behavioral reactions may include
- Nightmares or sleep disruptions
- Hypervigilance
- Increased startle response
- Emotional lability
- Increased conflict with family or coworkers
- Social isolation or withdrawal
- Increased use of alcohol or drugs
- Avoidance of trauma reminders

Emotional reactions may include
- Shock or disbelief
- Fear, anxiety, worry about safety of self and others
- Sadness, grief
- Feelings of helplessness and vulnerability
- Anger, rage, desire for vengeance
- Blame of self or others
- Survivor guilt
- Dissociation/depersonalization
- Numbness, disconnection

Cognitive reactions may include
- Confusion
- Reduced concentration and memory problems
- Amnesia (complete or partial)
- Flashbacks, intrusive thoughts and images
- Self-criticality and self-doubt
- Impaired decision making
- Focusing on protecting self and others
- Questioning spiritual/religious beliefs

Note: From *Mental health response to mass violence and terrorism: A training man*ual, by U.S. Department of Health and Human Services, DHHS Pub. No. SMA3959, 2004, Rockville, MD: Center for Mental Health Services, Substance Abuse and Mental Health Services Administration, 16–17.

reactions may occur occasionally, even years later; most people are likely to need support and provision of resources to ease the transition to normalcy; and some survivors may experience great distress and require community and at times clinical intervention (Galea et al., 2003; Watson, 2008).

Ongoing Response

Mental Health Agencies

When responding to a crisis involving a campus shooting the necessary mental health response will overwhelm the counseling center's staff. Thus, it is of critical importance to mobilize mental health responders who are on campus and off campus. An effective mobilization and organized response requires clarity about the leader or the department leading this response. The best choice to lead this response will be the counseling center director who will be able to have contact, and likely have previous relationships, with responders on and off campus.

On-campus participants include the following: psychology/counseling or discipline-related faculty, on-campus training clinic staff, the multicultural center's staff, employee assistance providers, and campus clergy. Off-campus resources should include the community mental health center, mental health association(s), the area university/college counseling center, the American Red Cross, and the state department of mental health.

Day 2 Response

The second day after the tragedy should begin with a debriefing meeting at the counseling center. Staff will be overwhelmed with what they experienced the previous day and will need a space to process their own reactions to be better prepared for the supportive work that will be required of them. Having regular debriefing meetings will be an asset to staff members as the center continues to provide support and recovery for the campus community. Extended hours for counseling should be provided, and this service should be announced to the campus community through the crisis response section of the university Web page.

Ongoing response will include the mobilization and deployment of on- and off-campus mental health providers. This coordination of mental health responders will be "necessary to reduce conflicts and potentially intrusive duplications of effort and to ensure appropriate services for survivors" (DHHS, 2004, p. 33). Prior to this component of the response efforts, the counseling center director, in collaboration with other university crisis response staff, should develop a plan for the provision of mental health services to the campus community. This plan should include locations and times that clinicians will be deployed and how acute crisis situations will be addressed.

In the initial deployment meeting with the mental health clinicians, several key elements must be covered. First, the counseling center director will assign clinician teams to specific populations they will serve and will outline parameters of the related service. Second, the plan for deployment and acute crisis management will be communicated. Third, clinicians should be instructed on how to interact with the media. It is advantageous to refer media to a central spokesperson (see p. 74 in chapter 3). Fourth, all volunteer clinicians should formally register and sign a liability release form. Finally, a follow-up meeting should be scheduled to facilitate continuity of care for all those receiving services.

As the response continues, two additional areas should be addressed. First, the mental health needs of the faculty and staff should be considered. The counseling center should work in concert with the campus employee assistance program or designated entity to ensure that the needs of faculty and staff are being met. Second, it is necessary to begin to focus on how to address the myriad mental health needs of the campus community when classes resume.

Campus Gatherings

Campus gatherings (e.g., impromptu vigils, memorials, etc.) provide an opportunity for the campus community to grieve collectively, to provide support for its members, and to begin to find hope in moving forward. It is important for counselors to be present at these events to provide support as needed. The mere presence of counselors can be of assistance to the campus community, but their presence should be subtle and in the background at these events. Similarly, counselors' advice related to the planning of these events should be nondirective, meaning they can provide guidance and support but should avoid leading the process. Allowing the campus community to take ownership for the planning is most effective, and clinicians can highlight areas of special concern for the event (DHHS, 2004).

Preparing Faculty and Staff to Return to Class

Intentional preparation of faculty and staff for the return of students is paramount to the campus community's healing process. As faculty and staff experience their own emotional reactions to the tragedy, they may have strong feelings about returning to work or the classroom. When individuals return to an area of mass violence, they may become extremely upset or overwhelmed (DHHS, 2004). Counselors should be prepared to assist faculty and staff who are anxious about students returning as well as about dealing with their own emotions. Particular attention should be paid to the faculty and staff who were more directly affected by the tragedy. For example, the academic department where the tragedy occurred, faculty who advise student groups that were directly affected, and individuals who lost a student or family member may require additional attention.

Outreach sessions or meetings should be provided for all faculty, staff, and graduate/teaching assistants prior to the resumption of classes. To accomplish this, heavy involvement from academic affairs will be necessary to communicate effectively the agenda and purpose of the sessions and to encourage attendance. Sessions should be organized by academic departments, allowing participants to attend sessions with their colleagues. Likewise, it will keep departments that were affected in different ways separate from one another, which provides a critical level of emotional safety for participants. In the case of a shooting, some faculty members may have known the shooter personally, as well as the victim(s); this dynamic will complicate emotional response. Faculty members who have students who were directly affected by the shooting (students killed or in the classroom) should be notified regarding those students. This information will allow them to be more prepared for absences when classes resume and to pay particular attention to students directly affected who return to class.

Sessions for faculty should be scheduled for 90 minutes to 2 hours and should be led by counselors with expertise in college student mental health and crisis work. The agenda should include information on grieving and crisis reactions (Kübler-Ross, 1969), mental health resources, and education about the classroom outreach program (discussed in the following section). Resources should be made available to participants (see the American Psychological Association's Help Center at http://www.APAhelpcenter.org for handout brochures and other materials) and should be distributed in multiple formats (e.g. hard copy, Web based, and e-mail). Most importantly, the formal agenda should be brief, allowing the majority of the time to be spent addressing questions and concerns and allowing participants to process their own reactions.

Classroom Outreach Program

Logistics

Placing a clinician in each class when courses resume will provide multiple benefits for faculty and students alike. Specifically, it will provide on-site support for students who experience various emotions upon returning to campus, and it will also assist faculty in addressing questions or concerns raised by students regarding the crisis. For most campuses, large or small, this type of classroom outreach program requires special preparation as well as the coordination of multiple volunteers. At a macro level, the goal should be to have one counselor in each class for the first 2 days of classes. This will provide coverage for classes that meet on alternate days. To maintain manageability, the counselor-to-student ratio should not exceed 1 to 100 (i.e., a lecture with 200 students requires a minimum of two counselors).

Calls and e-mails offering volunteer assistance will begin immediately and will come from many sources including other universities, private mental health professionals, clergy, and the general public. The crisis hotlines (see p. 74 in chapter 3) will receive most of these calls; hotline operators will require direction for organizing the information offered by prospective volunteers. To that end, a form should be created for hotline staff to collect predetermined information from those offering assistance, specifically clinicians. The form should include

➢ contact information (name, e-mail address, cell phone number, campus/agency, etc.)
➢ number of days the volunteer can assist, including arrival and departure times (It is important to note that volunteer time slots should be predetermined to cover class schedules; this will

provide more thorough classroom coverage, but may result in some volunteers being turned away as their availability does not match the scheduled slots.)

> volunteer's mobility issues, if any
> volunteer's other languages (including sign language)
> volunteer's professional license status

Hotline operators should be equipped with multiple copies of the form to complete as they answer the phone, and the form should also be available on the institution's Web site. If possible, potential volunteers should be able to submit the form directly online.

Some potential volunteers will contact staff members they already know and offer assistance. These individuals will provide some of the information required, but additional information will still be needed, making it necessary to contact volunteers directly. These potential volunteers should be contacted, thanked for their offer of assistance, and asked to complete the volunteer assistance form online.

At the same time the volunteer corps is being assembled, area hotels should be contacted to secure rooms for the clinicians. The local visitor's bureau or tourism office will be of assistance with this logistical task because of their preexisting relationships with area merchants. Securing rooms as quickly as possible is critical because media may descend on the campus and consume many of the rooms that will be needed.

The visitor's bureau may also be a good resource for contacting local restaurants. When the shooting occurred at Northern Illinois University, restaurants donated enough food to feed over 500 volunteers during their stay on campus. A solicitation letter/e-mail can be written ahead of time as part of your crisis management plan, making it possible to simply edit and send if necessary.

Another critical step in preparing for a crisis is meeting with the university's registrar to develop an understanding of the capabilities of your campus's software and a plan for scheduling volunteers. Determine if the registrar's data system has the ability to build volunteer schedules. Ideally, different types of schedules would be designed (e.g., 2 day or 1 day) that would align with the time slots offered on the volunteer assistance form. If this is not possible, work with your information technology department to identify staff members to assist with scheduling the volunteers. It will be vital to secure a master class schedule for the campus and to request the enrollment figure of each class so that appropriate coverage is scheduled. The registrar's office may have to alter the class schedule if the crisis affected a classroom space requiring it to be closed or taken off line for scheduling purposes (see chapter 7). Any change will initiate a domino effect through the schedule that will have an impact on volunteer assignments. It is critical that the team scheduling the volunteers be made aware of any changes to the master class schedule.

A specific issue that is more relevant to larger institutions is the placement of volunteer clinicians into zones. By dividing the campus into smaller regions or zones and assigning clinicians to a single zone, those who are unfamiliar with the campus will be able to better navigate their classroom assignments. Additionally, should volunteers have to cover classrooms not originally assigned to them, keeping the volunteers within their zone will ease their travel to the new assignment. The zoning of a campus is an important planning detail related to the scheduling of classes mentioned earlier; volunteer schedules should be confined to one zone for efficiency and effectiveness of the outreach effort.

Each zone should ideally have a hospitality center where counselors may wait between assignments and debrief with one another. If possible, providing any destressing activity, such as a massage therapist, is beneficial and will be appreciated. The hospitality centers also provide multiple locations for staging volunteers to cover any unforeseen schedule changes. Each hospitality center must have a phone, assigned staff from the university to coordinate volunteer efforts and answer questions, food and beverages, and message boards.

Finally, an orientation for all volunteer counselors will be necessary. In the crisis planning, identify three separate locations on campus that will accommodate the size of the volunteer group. This is necessary as one or more of the selected spaces may be reassigned for a different purpose. Conceptualize the orientation as a large conference. Provide a comfortable, warm, and dry area for registration and be mindful that the majority of volunteers will be arriving in a short period of time. To this end, check-in should be highly organized, well staffed, and provide enough room for queues inside. Networked computer(s) and a copier at registration will allow for on-site verification and making copies of volunteers' mental health licenses. The orientation should bring volunteers up to date on the crisis, review schedules and the purpose of the hospitality centers, address parking and transportation needs, and outline the role of the counselors in the classroom.

Psychological First Aid

The predominant role of the counselors in the classroom is to provide psychological first aid. The university community will be focusing on restoring the integrity of the learning environment, and psychological first aid will support and help to achieve that important goal. Students requiring individual mental health assistance should be escorted to the counseling center where they can meet with a counselor; having a counselor present in each class will facilitate these immediate referrals when indicated.

When working with individuals during and after a traumatic event, early contacts may help them alleviate painful emotions and encourage healing and recovery. Research, however, does not support the use of immediate debriefing with trauma survivors to reduce subsequent post-trauma symptoms, and the benefit of early and immediate use of cognitive behavioral treatments remains unproven. However, experts in the current empirical literature agree that "psychological first aid" is the early intervention of choice immediately after a traumatic event (Watson, 2008).

Psychological first aid has been defined as the use of pragmatic psychosocial interventions delivered during the first 4 weeks to individuals experiencing acute stress reactions or who may be experiencing problems in functioning, with the intent of aiding them in coping and problem solving (Young, 2006). The primary objectives include establishing safety, reducing extreme acute-stress-related responses, and when necessary, actively helping with problem solving and referrals. It should be tailored to the context, as a primary principle in providing psychological first aid is "respect for individual variation in recovering from trauma" (Watson, 2008, p. 77). Counselors should work toward meeting these objectives in the classroom, and how this can be accomplished should be discussed in the orientation session.

The National Center for Posttraumatic Stress Disorder and the National Child Traumatic Stress Network (NCPTSD, NCTSN; 2006) suggest a model that follows eight core actions: contact and engagement through response to requests for help as well as outreach efforts; provision of safety and comfort through physical and emotional support; stabilization to aid in calming those who may be overwhelmed (when necessary); information gathering about current needs and concerns; offering practical assistance when able; providing connection with social support; sharing information and education on stress reactions, coping, and trauma aftermath; and linking survivors with necessary services and providing referrals.

In colleges and universities, this approach means that clinicians should be ready not only to offer services in their counseling center setting but also to provide psychological first aid to groups and individuals across campus in various departments, organizations, and other common gathering places. It may also entail being able to provide information about community providers and other resources to assist in the recovery process. This means being prepared with information about clinicians in the local community, what services providers can offer, and whether they are able to serve students, faculty, and staff. The classroom outreach program will be a part of the eight core actions, and the process of achieving these steps should continue as the campus community moves forward.

Psychological first aid differs from traditional counseling and may require a slightly different skill set from what is used daily by some clinicians. Mental health responders who provide psychological first aid need to be able to rapidly assess survivors, to possibly shift away from conventional practice (e.g., to seek clients through providing outreach and community contact rather than waiting for survivors to request services), to provide care tailored to the context and culture of the survivors, to have a tolerance for strong expression of affect or symptomatic behavior, to be able to provide clear and concrete information, to be able to provide stabilization for someone in distress when needed, and to have the self-awareness to know when self-care is needed (Watson, 2008).

Sometimes those who are deployed in emergencies may not be able to meet all these criteria; however, during the orientation preparation, mental health responders can be introduced to the process and will have a better sense of what to expect. Those who are responsible for the coordination of responders can structure how care is delivered to incorporate some of the core actions suggested by the NCPTSD and the NCTSN. For example, teams of responders may be visibly located in the campus community after a crisis, thereby encouraging responders to seek out those in need of attention.

Psychoeducation

A key component of psychological first aid is psychoeducation, which can occur as a part of the classroom outreach project to help normalize the recovery process and promote healing. In providing psychological first aid in the classroom, counselors will also be providing psychoeducation about the healing process. Psychoeducation involves sharing key information and educating the target population on common stress reactions to trauma. Education demystifies the healing process, and allows those affected to better understand their own experience and hopefully regain a greater sense of control and efficacy (Young, 2006). Mental health responders should use their judgment regarding whether and when to present information to survivors, since some individuals may perceive educational efforts as suggestions of symptoms they should have, or they may not be emotionally ready to learn about trauma reactions (Young). It is also important for clinicians to remember that comments to survivors may set a premature timeline for recovery (e.g., Why haven't you gotten over this yet?) as well as negative self-critical self-perceptions by survivors (e.g., Why haven't I gotten over this yet?); both scenarios are associated with increased rates of post-traumatic stress disorder (PTSD; Watson, 2008). It is important that clinicians keep in mind that psychoeducation is most effective when mental health responders adapt their comments and materials to each survivor's style and needs (DHHS, 2004).

Long-Term Implications and Other Considerations

Psychological Effects of Trauma

The classroom outreach program will provide information, resources, and hopefully assist the campus community in beginning the journey toward healing and recovery. The process of healing from a campus crisis will be unique to the individual, and this process is affected by the psychological effects of the trauma. There are some basic assumptions, founded on research as well as clinical experience, that point to how the psychological effects of trauma might be manifested immediately, as well as years later, following a traumatic event (Flynn & Heitzmann, 2008; Jones, 2006). Employing the Population Exposure Model (DHHS, 2004; Tucker et al., 1999), one can assume that those most directly affected would be those who suffer from acute stress disorder and PTSD. However, individuals who are more socially isolated and who, because of their background, may be more psychologically vulnerable, would have greater difficulty finding the social support they would need after traumatic events. These individuals could also be assumed to require psychological assistance, even if not directly affected by an event. This means that there may be many more individuals needing psychological assistance than initially expected, and that the ripples of a crisis have the potential to be felt across a campus community over time.

Campus communities that have suffered a crisis might also find themselves with a higher base level of anxiety and distress, affecting various constituencies beyond those directly affected. For example, at Virginia Tech, a survey shortly after the shootings in April 2007 found that at least 5% of students reported significant symptoms of PTSD, and an additional 21% of students reported symptoms consistent with an elevated risk for PTSD. In the same survey, faculty and staff reported 3% and 17%, respectively (Flynn & Heitzmann, 2008). These numbers, as well as similar studies post-9/11 in New York City (see, for example, Galea et al., 2003), point to how mental health repercussions after a trauma are often felt beyond those directly affected, and how a "list of victims" will not cover all the individuals who have been exposed and affected by an event (Raphael, 2008).

With the potential for such a wide-ranging impact, along with a heightened sensitivity to trauma, administrators will be wise to provide increased counseling resources on campus post-trauma through adding positions in their counseling centers as well as developing specific resources for those directly affected. There will be a heightened need to develop a postcrisis plan to identify and address the needs of priority populations; likewise, an appropriate service delivery system will have to be developed to support the protection of the community's mental health as well as that of the providers.

Interagency Agreements

Resources can include what a university can provide as well as those provided by community and governmental partners. Triaging requests for services is an important part of ensuring that resources will be available to victims over a sustained time frame. Established relationships with outside agencies will assist a counseling center that is responding to a campus crisis.

Specifically, the development of interagency agreements with other mental health facilities will provide efficient delivery of services and other necessary support for the campus community in the event of a crisis. Advance awareness of procedures for bringing external clinicians to campus to provide services is an important aspect of the crisis planning process. Establishing collaborative relationships and protocols in advance will assist the mental health response to a campus crisis; focusing on the development of these relationships and the related protocol should be a part of the crisis management planning.

Ethical and Legal Considerations

The ability to communicate openly about traumatic incidents on campus also can be affected by legal and ethical concerns. While the confidentiality of what is shared in counseling must be protected, at times other campus stakeholders may ask for more information about a student involved in a particular event. If the student is/has been a client at a counseling center, clinicians should be aware how to manage requests for information from outside the center while also protecting individual clients. At times this may mean offering hypothetical information or serving solely as a consultant to provide expertise without compromising an individual's confidentiality (Flynn & Heitzmann, 2008).

Further complications may arise after a crisis should legal action be taken by parties affected and/or their families. If a student in treatment is involved in legal action, this potentially can complicate already established counseling relationships. These students who are being treated by the institution's counseling center may also be plaintiffs in a case against that institution. Clinicians working with such students should be aware of the possible complication and consult with their director as well as with legal counsel about how to proceed in an ethical fashion.

State laws related to mental health vary, and ethics codes for mental health providers typically demand a certain standard for protecting confidentiality, yet each state's laws may dictate how confidentiality is managed. What happens related to confidentiality postmortem can be an issue that emerges postcrisis. In certain states, confidentiality may transfer to the estate of the deceased, and this may in turn affect how information is released and shared. In other states, confidentiality may be maintained and stay with an individual postmortem and not shift to the deceased's estate. Checking with legal counsel regarding these distinctions can be crucial.

After a campus crisis, another potential challenge relates to fact gathering. For example, law enforcement agencies may be involved in ascertaining events that led up to the trauma, especially when the trauma is crime related. This means that staff in various departments may find themselves having to deal with managing search warrants or subpoenas.

Search warrants are issued by judges or clerk magistrates whenever a law enforcement official supplies a sworn allegation of probable cause. A search warrant authorizes law enforcement officers to search designated premises, motor vehicles, or people, and to seize specific evidence relating to a criminal investigation. A search warrant is the functional equivalent of a court order. It must be obeyed, leaving for subsequent court proceedings any challenge to the lawfulness of the warrant and the admissibility of the fruits of the search that the warrant authorized (Angeli, Ramfjord, Sim, & Rosenbaum, 2006).

A subpoena is a court order and stipulates the appearance of a person or the production of certain records or things. Subpoenas may be issued by either party in civil and criminal proceedings. Failure to obey a subpoena may constitute contempt of court, which can result in imposition of a fine, a jail term, or both; however, one should be aware that unlike a search warrant, a subpoena may be open to inquiry, and one can possibly negotiate with the court regarding the amount and scope of information released. A subpoena may be broader in scope initially since there is not yet sufficient evidence for a warrant; however, it is important to work to limit that scope and protect as best one can confidential and privileged information. The goal is to cooperate as much as possible with a subpoena to avoid having a search warrant issued (Angeli et al., 2006).

If served with either a search warrant or subpoena, especially after a crisis in which it appears that evidence is being collected, it is advisable to seek legal counsel. These documents should be reviewed to ensure legitimacy and to ensure they do not overstep boundaries nor allow for additional searches. If information is seized, an inventory of what is taken should be made in the event that it may have significance in the future. Campus employees interviewed under these situations should only do so with legal counsel present to protect their rights (Angeli et al., 2006).

Self-Care

Immediately after an event, on-campus resources such as the counseling center will surely experience increased use. The multiple demands on a campus counseling center have the potential to ultimately burn out staff if not managed appropriately. The energy that staff members expend to provide assistance for others will deplete their own personal energy level. Mental health staff members who respond to acts of mass violence need systematic and comprehensive stress management (Center for Mental Health Services, 2001). The counseling center leadership must evaluate how long counselors can provide services and whether some job tasks should be reprioritized or limited (DHHS, 2004). In the absence of appropriate personal stress management and monitoring of workload, staff members may suffer compassion fatigue.

Compassion fatigue is the result of intense work that drains the empathy from the counselor, resulting in the experience of negative symptoms (Figley, 1995). An effective stress management program should be established to avoid negative consequences from the work counselors will provide. An effective program will include management of workload, a balanced lifestyle, strategies for stress reduction, and self-awareness (DHHS, 2004). Encouraging staff members to engage in self-care will enhance the environment in the counseling center, enhance productivity, and improve the quality of services provided to students.

The work required of the counseling center staff after a crisis event will be intense and highly complex. Clinicians will be challenged in ways they had not previously experienced. Ensuring that counseling center staff members are mindful of their own needs will benefit the staff, the students they serve, and the campus community at large.

Conclusion

The mental health issues present on college and university campuses are having a direct impact on the work of the university counseling center. A significant part of this work has become responding to crisis events on campus, which involves significant planning, attention to details, and collaboration. The mental health response will encapsulate short- and long-term action steps.

The mental health response will be taxing for those involved in the leadership, execution, and clinical provision of the response. The magnitude of the response is inherently what makes it so difficult for the counseling center staff. Staff members will be performing duties outside the center's normal daily operations to meet the comprehensive needs of the campus community.

Finally, the uniqueness of each college or university campus should be stressed. A one-size-fits-all approach will not serve each institution in responding to a campus crisis. The information contained in this chapter should be used as a guide, and the specifics of responding should be edited to match each institution. Preparing and responding to a crisis in an institution-specific manner will provide the accurate support that the campus needs to move forward.

References

Angeli, D., Ramfjord, P. A., Sim, J. R., & Rosenbaum, L. O. (2006). *Stoel Rives' White-Collar Crime Breakfast Series presentation: What to do when the FBI knocks on your door.* Retrieved from http:// http://www.stoel.com/files/WhiteCollarSeries2.pdf

Bell, C. C. (2008). Should culture considerations influence early intervention? In M. Blumenfield & R. J. Ursano (Eds.), *Intervention and resilience after mass trauma* (pp. 127–148). Cambridge, UK: Cambridge University Press.

Center for Mental Health Services. (2001). [Interviews with state and local experts: Mental health response and recovery following incidents of mass criminal victimization and presidentially declared disasters.] Unpublished raw data.

Figley, C. R. (Ed.). (1995). *Compassion fatigue: Coping with secondary traumatic stress disorder in those who treat the traumatized.* New York: Brunner/Mazel.

Flynn, B. W., & Norwood, A. E. (2004). Defining normal psychological reactions to disaster. *Psychiatric Annals, 34*(8), 597–603.

Flynn, C., & Heitzmann, D. (2008) Tragedy at Virginia Tech: Trauma and its aftermath. *The Counseling Psychologist, 36*(3), 479–489.

Galea, S., Vlahov, D., Resnick, H., Ahern, J., Susser, E., Gold, J., Bucuvalas, M., & Kilpatrick, D. (2003). Trends of probable post-traumatic stress disorder in New York City after the September 11 terrorist attacks. *American Journal of Epidemiology, 158*(6), 514–524.

Gallagher, R. (2008). *National survey of counseling center directors 2008.* Alexandria, VA: International Association of Counseling Services.

Howe, N., & Strauss, W. (2003). *Millennials go to college: Strategies for a new generation on campus: Recruiting and admissions, campus life, and the classroom.* Washington, DC: American Association of Collegiate Registrars and Admissions Officers.

Jones, R. (2006). *Public health response to Hurricanes Katrina and Rita: Applying lessons learned to mental health/substance abuse needs.* Retrieved June 10, 2009, from http://www.apa.org/divisions/div45/images/jones_presentation.pdf

Kübler-Ross, E. (1969). *On death and dying: What the dying have to teach doctors, nurses, clergy, and their own families.* New York: Simon & Schuster.

National Center for Posttraumatic Stress Disorder & National Child Traumatic Stress Network. (2006). *Psychological first aid: Field operations guide* (2nd ed.). Rockville, MD: Center for Mental Health Services, Substance Abuse, and Mental Health Services Administration.

Norris, F. H., Friedman, M. J., & Watson, P. J. (2002). 60,000 disaster victims speak: Part 2, summary and implications of the disaster mental health research. *Psychiatry, 65*(3), 240–261.

Raphael, B. (2008). Systems, science, and populations. In M. Blumenfield & R. J. Ursano (Eds.), *Intervention and resilience after mass trauma* (pp. 1–48). Cambridge, UK: Cambridge University Press.

Tucker, P., Pferrerbaum, B., Nixon, S. J., & Foy, D. W. (1999). Trauma and recovery among adults highly exposed to a community disaster. *Psychiatric Annals, 29*(2), 78–83.

U.S. Department of Health and Human Services. (2004). *Mental health response to mass violence and terrorism: A training manual* (DHHS Publication No. SMA3959). Rockville, MD: Center for Mental Health Services, Substance Abuse, and Mental Health Services Administration.

Watson, P. J. (2008). Psychological first aid. In M. Blumenfield & R. J. Ursano (Eds.), *Intervention and resilience after mass trauma* (pp. 69–84). Cambridge, UK: Cambridge University Press.

Young, B. H. (2006). The immediate response to disaster: Guidelines for adult psychological first aid. In E. C. Ritchie, P. J. Watson, & M. J. Friedman (Eds.), *Interventions following mass violence and disasters: Strategies for mental health practice* (pp. 134–154). New York: Guildford Press.

5 Essential Student Affairs Services in a Campus Crisis

*James E. Brunson III, Michael Stang,
and Angela Dreessen*

IN THE late 1980s Michael Clay Smith (1989) warned that violence is a reality on college campuses. Between the 1970s and 1990s, campus marches, sit-ins, draft card burnings, and riots escalated to sexual and aggravated assaults, serious property crimes, robberies, and homicides. Dispelling the common notion of a college campus as a type of sanctuary from the troubles of the world, Smith emphasized higher education's duty to provide protective measures and to respond appropriately following troublesome incidents. Unfortunately, these efforts have been insufficient to eliminate increasingly serious situations on today's college campuses. In response to ongoing concerns about campus violence across the country, strong essential services on today's campuses require proactive approaches (Jackson, Terrell, & Heard, 2007; Smith & Fossey, 1995).

Smith's (1989) account demonstrates the importance of strong essential services programs. Student affairs professionals are constantly examining best practices at institutions of all sizes and types. After the shooting at Virginia Tech (April 2007), representatives of 288 institutions of higher education across the nation indicated in a survey that they had conducted a review of their crisis response plans (Rasmussen & Johnson, 2008). Approaches to threat assessment, communication, enhanced counseling services, case management strategies, and emergency response protocols are shared regularly by some institutions.

This chapter is designed to provide information about the role of essential services in responding to a crisis. For the purpose of this chapter, essential services include, but are not limited to, housing and dining, student activities, and international student services (Barr & Associates, 1988; Lambert, 2002); depending on the culture of an individual campus, other departments could easily be considered essential in nature. The chapter specifically focuses on the process of crisis management as well as recovery and healing initiatives that are the catalyst for reclamation of the campus after a crisis (Jablonski, McClellan, & Zdziarski, 2009).

Defining and Developing Policy for Essential Services

Lack of preparation, planning, and ability to manage a crisis is not an option for institutions of higher education. Campus shootings have brought national attention to college policies and response plans, and best practices include identifying and preparing essential services providers long before an incident occurs (Committee on Education and Labor, 2007). Essential student services are defined as offices, departments, and personnel leveraged in responding to crisis situations. While some essential services focus on immediate crisis management, other student services attend to the healing and recovery process. Essential student services may vary slightly depending on institutional structure, demographics, and culture.

When determining the function and impact of essential services in crisis situations, it is important that student affairs leadership provide general guidelines for offices, units, and personnel. Such guidelines may already exist and could be internal departmental policies. A centralized essential services policy for a division outlines a comprehensive distribution and communication plan that permits staff members to know in advance what roles they will play during a crisis (Zdziarski et al., 2007).

While essential services directors find themselves responding to departmental policies and procedures, they might be called upon to support broader institutional needs. Managing crisis events might even require that staff members assume leadership roles and responsibilities that go beyond their job descriptions.

Student affairs professionals manage programs and resources that often help to move the campus community beyond tragedy and toward healing and recovery; however, when the aftereffect of a mass campus shooting escalates, the heightened demand for staff expertise and time intensifies. For that reason, attention must be given to how essential services providers respond to unfolding events and their impact on staff members. Directors must be cognizant of fellow employees' emotional states, be sensitive to their personal needs, be supportive and attentive, and respond appropriately. This awareness must also include paraprofessionals, particularly undergraduate and graduate student staff members. Many student affairs departments have student employees who manage daily operations. In the days following a campus crisis, it is important to gauge employees' emotional state to ensure that they are ready to return to work. Some staff members might view direct involvement and engagement as contributing to the healing and recovery process. Plans that offer a variety of opportunities for all levels and types of staff to contribute in a meaningful way should be developed, and rotating schedules and intentional breaks, especially for staff in high demand, should also be included (Duncan & Miser, 2000).

Housing and Dining

During a crisis, the housing and dining unit provides essential services that residents find reassuring. Housing and dining often comprises three functional areas: residential life, residential operations, and residential dining. These areas represent a variety of configurations including residence halls, on-campus apartments, university-owned houses, and in some cases Greek-letter facilities. In addition to student residents, housing and dining might maintain summer conference operations that serve thousands of nonstudent residents.

Residential life staff members must be thoroughly trained for service provider roles. During a crisis, residential living should provide safety and security, furnish meals, offer activities and programs, and supply other resources crucial to healing and recovery. Security priorities require collaborative partnerships with campus police or other law enforcement agencies. Safety-check protocols should require limited building access, periodic walk-throughs, strict adherence to guest policies, and communication updates. Student residents would benefit from updates through departmental Web sites, e-mail, text messages, signage/posters, and hall/floor meetings.

Creating a partnership with the campus counseling center and religious organizations in advance will enable the unit to anticipate ongoing healing and recovery initiatives. In this regard, temporary counseling centers within the residential communities provide vital support. A generally accepted practice on most college campuses is that the counseling center responds to crisis situations, and team members are deployed to strategic locations (see chapter 4). Furthermore, members of the clergy with pastoral or counseling training would offer crucial resources and support as well.

University officials might also request and encourage students to vacate the college campus until an incident has been resolved. Unfortunately, many students living on campus may view residential housing as their permanent home; they may even lack the necessary resources to depart. In addition, while most residential housing follows the traditional academic calendar, students on some college campuses remain in residential housing year-round. As a result, student housing- and dining-related facilities are almost always an essential service and may play an especially significant role should *shelter-in-place* protocols become necessary. Shelter-in-place protocols are safe and secure residential environments on campus. Housing units are practical choices for shelter locations because they are designed to manage and maintain large numbers of people.

In general, residential dining is either self-operated or contracted with outside vendors. While typically functioning during the academic year, some food service operations also serve summer conference programs. Dining facilities may be physically attached to housing/residential complexes, student union buildings, or other campus facilities that regularly provide meals or cater special events. During a crisis of extended duration, dining operations may collaborate to service students, families, and university employees. Collaborative partnerships, and in some cases prearranged business agreements, must be in place for these essential services to function effectively.

Student Activities

The staff of the student activities department could be called upon to take the lead in crisis-related program planning and implementation. Programmatic initiatives may be requested by campus officials that promote campus community healing and recovery (see chapter 6). These initiatives serve a number of purposes: They provide students with information and emotional support, provide opportunities for all community members to pay their respects to the victims, and provide access to other resources. The campus community will also need outlets to express its grief and initiate the long healing and recovery process. Campus-wide healing initiatives might include campus vigils, moments of silence, ribbon campaigns, and memorial services. Staff members might also manage smaller events specific to student organizations.

As the immediate crisis situation recedes, and the focus shifts to recovery and healing efforts, inclusive program efforts will depend on the nature of the campus culture, student body, and community members. Student activities staff should work closely with college administrators to provide programs and services for the community that has been affected by the crisis. Additionally, student activities staff should work with the counseling center to ensure the appropriate tone and level of respect to accommodate different styles of grieving.

Typically, members of the student activities department have the most direct contact with student organizations. A crisis can have an impact on student groups, particularly those whose members are directly involved in a campus shooting. The student activities department must provide outreach services and resources to those groups. Under such circumstances, advising can take on new meaning as well. Staff advisers should anticipate the need to be available for their students and seek out any advice and support from other colleagues as needed.

In day-to-day operations, student activities often serves as a liaison between students and administrators. Following a traumatic event, this role is especially important and needs to be handled carefully because of its sensitive nature. Ongoing, open communication with student leadership will be important, as student leaders may assume ownership of support and recovery initiatives. Therefore, it is critical to keep them involved and feeling that they are being heard by administration throughout the process.

Community members might seek meaningful ways to contribute to the healing process, and it is important for the institution to provide an outlet. Projects may range from selling items to planning memorial concerts. While some external entities may be honest and well intentioned, other outside groups might try to profit from the situation. For example, the institution's logo and image may need to be protected from profiteers and projects viewed by members of the university community as offensive. It is important to coordinate this work with appropriate offices or divisional representatives to manage activities and protect the institution's integrity. Collaborative relationships ensure respect and sensitivity toward those most deeply affected.

Following their campus tragedies, Virginia Tech (April 2007) and Northern Illinois University (February 2008) held public memorial programs to acknowledge the grief and loss felt by everyone, to support the families that lost their children, and to help the students, faculty, staff, and community prepare for a return to classes and campus life. Implementing large-scale events in a very short timeline is a highly difficult task; therefore, forethought related to crisis planning extends to these programmatic initiatives as well.

Program content will vary depending on the nature of the crisis and community needs; however, maintaining a detailed account of facilities and venues available for use at various times of the year, and plans for accessing high-quality sound, stage, and lighting resources will greatly assist the program planning process when it is needed most. At Virginia Tech, for instance, the crisis occurred toward the end of the spring semester. The university's location and time of year allowed it to hold its memorial ceremony outdoors. At Northern Illinois the crisis occurred during a cold weather month requiring indoor venues. Because of logistical issues, student activities professionals must consider a range of options and develop base plans accordingly.

International Student Services

The international student services department provides culturally sensitive programs and resources to international students, scholars, and faculty members during times of crisis. Services include special translation services, immigration services, support in dealing with insurance, or assistance with repatriation or medical evacuation. Precautions must be taken to ensure that no campus office inadvertently reveals the immigration status of any victims, friends, or family members of students, scholars, or faculty members affected by campus violence. It is important to remember that because of the time and resources needed in planning travel, most international students cannot go home immediately. For international faculty and students, canceling an entire academic semester could have serious repercussions. If the campus shuts down partially or completely, they will need support services. And because international populations often rely on public transportation, special attention should be given to the challenges of students living in off-campus housing.

International student services may also provide services to students studying abroad and may extend support to their parents and families. Communication with students studying abroad is critical. Telephone, text and e-mail messaging, as well as social networking technologies permit students studying abroad to follow events in real time.

The potential global implications of the crisis incident management process bears consideration. The international student services department helps the campus community understand the impact on nonimmigrants and students studying abroad. Staff members serve as a contact point for consulates and embassies, providing them with relevant and timely information that is essential to international students and students studying abroad. Collaborative relationships provide support and resources for these special populations for responding and reacting to tragic events (Neidermeyer & Terjesen, 2008).

Conclusion

This chapter highlights essential services needed in responding to a campus crisis. Specific roles, functions, and use of staff and resources in departments and offices such as housing and dining, student activities, and international student services are defined. Additionally, partnerships between essential services departments and other campus units and community agencies are emphasized. Of course, all student affairs departments and professionals can be integral in crisis response, but thoughtful preplanning and preparation for these units can greatly enhance student services during a campus crisis.

References

Barr, M. J., & Associates. (1988). *Student services and the law: A handbook for practitioners.* San Francisco: Jossey-Bass.

Committee on Education and Labor. (2007). *Best practices for making college campuses safe: Hearing before the Committee on Education and Labor, 110th Congress, first session, hearing held in Washington, DC, May 15, 2007.* Washington, DC: U.S. Government Printing Office.

Duncan, M. A., & Miser, K. M. (2000). *Dealing with campus crisis.* In M. J. Barr, M. K. Desler, & Associates (Eds.), *The handbook of student affairs administration* (pp. 453–474). San Francisco: Jossey-Bass.

Jablonski, M. A., McClellan, G., & Zdziarski, E. L. (Eds.). (2009). *In search of safer communities: Practices for student affairs in addressing campus violence.* Washington, DC: Student Affairs Administrators in Higher Education.

Jackson, J. F. L., Terrell, M. C., & Heard, R. L. (2007). *Creating and maintaining safe college campuses: A sourcebook for enhancing and evaluating safety programs.* Sterling, VA: Stylus.

Lambert, L. M. (2002). Chief academic officers. In R. Diamond (Ed.), *Field guide to academic leadership* (pp. 425–436). San Francisco: Jossey-Bass.

Neidermeyer, P. E., & Terjesen, S. (2008). Shots heard around the world: Campus violence and international student concerns. In M. A Paludi (Ed.), *Understanding and preventing campus violence* (pp. 41–50). New York: Praeger.

Rasmussen, C., & Johnson, G. (2008). *The ripple effect of Virginia Tech: Assessing the nationwide impact on campus safety and security policy and practice.* Minneapolis: Midwestern Higher Education Compact.

Smith, M. C. (1989, fall). The ancestry of campus violence. *New Directions for Student Services, 47,* 5–11.

Smith, M. C., & Fossey, W. R. (1995). *Crime on campus: Legal issues and campus administration.* Phoenix, AZ: Oryx Press.

Zdziarski, E., Dunkel, N., Rollo, J., & Associates. (2007). *Campus crisis management: A comprehensive guide to planning, prevention, response, and recovery.* San Francisco: Jossey-Bass.

6 Healing Your Community

Kelly S. Wesener, Scott Peska, and Monica Treviño

"TRAGEDY IS the author of hope. Crisis brings us face to face with our soul" (Bolman & Deal, 1995, p. 35). The care and support of the campus community displayed in the aftermath of a tragedy reveals the strength, resolve, and true character of an institution. Sandeen (2006) said, "An institution . . . rarely, if ever, reveals itself to be something different during a crisis. . . . Its 'soul' is there in place. . . . A crisis reveals what an institution's values are" (p. 66). This chapter focuses on how colleges and universities have and will continue to receive comfort and provide care in the days, weeks, months, and years following a senseless, horrific act of violence.

An institution can provide an endless number of responses to assist in the community's healing process and to refocus on the educational mission of the institution. It is important to note there is no consensus in the literature regarding best practices or effective interventions in the immediate or intermediate period following a crisis (Gersons & Olff, 2005). Each traumatic event is holistically different in its severity and in the resiliency of its community. Research in the area of crisis intervention does, however, provide some insights into effective strategies to restore a culture and support the members of the community. Hobfoll et al. (2007) list five key elements that should be included in all immediate and midterm crisis interventions. University officials should promote a sense of safety, calm, self-efficacy and community efficacy, connectedness, and hope. Research also shows that following a traumatic event, rituals assist in "reestablishing feelings of control, belonging, and social solidarity within and beyond one's immediate community" (Eyre, 2006, p. 442). Additionally, acceptance of the changes brought about by crisis is enhanced with the opportunity to remember, mourn, and

reconnect with the community (Herman, 1992). Many of the immediate responses noted throughout this book naturally create a sense
of calm and safety. With that understanding, this chapter focuses on
responses that provide a community with a sense of self-efficacy and
community efficacy, connectedness, and hope.

A University Provides Opportunities to Heal

Community expressions following a disaster "are an important part
of grief and mourning. . . . Recovery requires a sense of social community in which people feel supported in looking back and forward"
(Eyre, 2006, p. 454). An important component in the university's
crisis response is providing opportunities for members of the community to gather and to express themselves in mourning. These expressions of mourning can take many forms with varying degrees of
formality and planning.

Community gatherings can be powerful events for an institution
in crisis. Researchers "have reinforced the significance of social support for those who are traumatized, including the value of social
responses to death, grief, and mourning" (Eyre, 2006, p. 443), and
these gatherings provide that opportunity. Not only do they allow the
members of a community to be with one another, but they also provide an opportunity for all the people at the university to see their
president and institutional leadership not on the television or computer screen but speaking directly to them. Candlelight vigils in the
aftermath of a tragedy have become a ritual in our society. These
gatherings often are impromptu and other times are organized by the
institution such as the one in 1999 at the site of the bonfire that
collapsed at Texas A&M University when over 40,000 people lit candles and observed silence for up to 2 hours (Whitmarsch, 1999).

In addition to community gatherings, providing a space for personal reflection is another simple but important resource for a healing community. At institutions that may not have a campus chapel, a
quiet room designated for reflection can be used. According to Eyre
(2006), "Designating a location for group or personal meditation,
whether permanent or temporary, can help people heal" (p. 447).

Another space for reflection can be found in the written word. Within 24 hours of a shooting at one institution, campus administrators placed message boards in the center of the campus. These boards not only offered a place for expression but also provided a location for people to gather and connect with others struggling with the effects of the tragedy. As Eyre (2006) points out, "Advances in technology and increasing use of the Internet have resulted in the development of virtual memorials" (p. 452). Web sites and online journals provide an opportunity for expression also. At Virginia Tech, 36,000 entries were made in an online journal by individuals and groups offering their condolences for the victims of the shooting in April 2007.

The practice of "remembering in silence" (Eyre, 2006, p. 448) is centuries old, and it remains a meaningful way a community can reflect, observe, and unite after a campus tragedy. Northern Illinois University, 7 days to the minute after its shooting tragedy, commemorated the event with 5 minutes of silence.

Many institutions provide memorial services for loss of any life in the campus community.

> Formal memorial services often follow some time after the initial aftermath of the communal tragedies, allowing for a more extended period of time for planning and organization. Their location, formality, and content symbolize the sense, scale, and significance of the communal loss. (Eyre, 2006, p. 450)

The memorial service at Virginia Tech was not only a ritual of healing for the campus, it was also an international event broadcast live worldwide. Because of the public nature of this type of event, the institution must use adequate time, staff, and resources to make sure the university is appropriately represented. Knowing that the service is very public, exceptional care should be taken regarding the families of the victims and those who survived the incident. A special reception prior to or after the event allows families to interact with one another and institutional leaders to express their condolences in a more intimate setting.

It is important to commemorate milestones. Community expressions can "mark the transitions of time and status for individuals and the community" (Eyre, 2006, p. 455). The passing of 365 days after a shooting is a milestone for the institution and the community.

> In the same way as formal memorial services conducted shortly after a tragedy fulfill both psychological and social functions, so do anniversary events. They mark the passage of social and chronological time as well as the impetus and long journey toward community rehabilitation and recovery. (p. 451)

The commemorative events must balance respect for the victims, honor the resilience of the survivors, and recognize the hope and rebuilding manifested during the previous year. Involving the campus and greater community in planning the events is an opportunity to continue to strengthen relationships across and beyond the campus. Administrators at Virginia Tech and Northern Illinois University provided a full day of events designed to offer opportunities for memorial expressions in many forms, including musical performances, art displays, multifaith services, rooms for reflection, and a reception where injured students, victims' families, and the university's leadership had the opportunity to formally thank the emergency personnel who were first on the scene. On this day, events and traditions can be established that will be carried forward at the annual commemoration of the tragedy for years to come. This is an important time for solidarity and remembrance.

Graduation is an annual milestone at every university. The conferring of posthumous degrees upon those lost in the tragedy is another opportunity for reflection and healing for the campus community as it convenes during this significant ritual.

A Community Expresses Itself

Expressions of grief will naturally occur in a variety of forms, many impromptu and unplanned by the university. According to Eyre (2006), "Spontaneous expressions of grief are now the rule rather than the exception following sudden, tragic death in, for example, fatal road crashes, acts of murder, and disasters" (p. 443).

Public memorial sites have become commonplace—roadside crosses mark the location of an accident that took a life, and flowers, teddy bears, and pictures collect near the site of a tragedy. Campuses experiencing gun violence are no exception. Within 24 hours of the shooting at Virginia Tech, a student group placed 32 Hokie stones for the victims slain. Five crosses on a hill just beyond the shooting site at Northern Illinois University memorialize the five students who lost their lives. These locations became the communities' temporary memorial sites with mourners leaving thousands of items behind as expressions of grief.

In its darkest hour the campus community will be sustained by an outpouring of support from around the world. Thousands of cards, letters, and banners expressing condolences will pour into the university. Expressions of grief come in all shapes, sizes, and sometimes in large volume. All the items sent to universities must be received, distributed, or stored in the midst of the crisis. Some items come with specific instructions regarding their use and distribution. Respecting these expectations and managing the sheer number of contributions can "become management challenges for those tasked with organizing" during a crisis (Eyre, 2006, p. 444).

Comfort quilts have become an expression of support sent to places that have experienced large-scale tragedies and have become a national symbol for those who have survived a crisis. One such quilt was made by students from St. Hilary Catholic School in Fairlawn, Virginia, after the tragedy in New York City on 9/11, the quilt was next sent to New Orleans after Hurricane Katrina, then to the Nickel Mines Amish School in Pennsylvania after a shooting there in 2006, and was later passed to Northern Illinois University by Virginia Tech. It is a treasured gift that hopefully has found its permanent home.

Local Community Support

In an effort to support the university, people and businesses in surrounding communities will make donations to the institution, monetary and material. Local restaurants may provide food for staff members who are working around the clock; shopping centers may provide basics such as bottled water and boxes of tissues. Many area vendors will offer items needed for the numerous activities on the campus such as ribbons and pins to support a remembrance ribbon campaign, candles for the vigils, and flowers for the podium at the memorial service. Any requests by the university are quickly accommodated by the community and will help offset the unanticipated expenses of managing the tragedy.

In addition to support from beyond the institution, religious communities can play a key role in the recovery process. Following a tragedy, local religious centers and clergy members can provide support in many ways by conducting services, ceremonies, and prayer rituals in their faith communities; offering emotional support for faculty, staff, and students; finding shelter for international students or those who have no home to return to; and hosting dinners for students when dining services are closed. Clergy also provide support to families at local hospitals, using their already established relationships with the hospital staff and administration. Spiritual leaders may also staff hospitality rooms for families on campus. To effectively use the resources provided by faith communities, a university staff member should be assigned as a liaison to work with religious leaders who are providing outreach and support to those affected by the shooting.

Finally, a public display of community support is often shown by collegiate and professional sports teams. The New York Yankees baseball team visited Virginia Tech on the first anniversary of the shooting and played the university's baseball team, a true morale booster for the community. After the shooting at Northern Illinois University, the Chicago White Sox honored those lost by inviting the college president to throw the first pitch at the season's opening baseball game. Some professional and collegiate teams support communities in crisis by wearing an affected university's logo on their hats or uniforms.

Issues of Sensitivity

A number of factors should be considered in planning and implementing events that facilitate the grieving process.

It is important for a campus community to recognize that its members will want to contribute to the healing. Finding meaningful opportunities for the community to "do something" will be significant to those individuals. Giving small but necessary tasks to staff, such as folding event programs or setting up chairs for seating at an event, will allow community members to make their own contributions to the recovery process. Volunteers can assist by making memorial lapel ribbons that are not only small tokens of remembrance but also a step forward in the healing process. As Sandeen (2006) said, "When staff members find ways to be helpful in a crisis, they grow professionally, and the staff's sense of community is enhanced. Positions and titles are usually quite unimportant in this situation; every person should be . . . invited to participate" (p. 65).

Fund-Raising as a Support Mechanism

Many affected by the tragedy in and outside the campus community will want to reach out to the institution with financial support. Fund-raising is a supportive effort from the community that may bring with it numerous considerations. Who is collecting the money and are they perceived as representing the university, even if the institution is unaware of their efforts? Is there a record of who contributed, how much money was given, and are there specific earmarks for the funds? Are the fund-raising efforts in line with the institution's regulations and protocols? In addition, some individuals and groups will create their own items (magnets, ribbons, T-shirts, etc.) to sell in an effort to raise funds. Do these items fall within the university's guidelines regarding the use of institutional branded images? Misunderstandings between the institution, the donor, and those with good intentions for raising funds can bring about further strains in already difficult circumstances. Colleges and universities may want to set up designated accounts or scholarship funds that will be used in the event of unexpected giving. Establishing guidelines and protocols prior to a large-scale event can ensure institutional integrity in fund-raising efforts, regardless of whether those efforts are conducted from within or outside the institution. This will require a working partnership with a number of campus offices that might include institutional advancement, alumni relations, community outreach, public relations, and university business offices.

If a scholarship is established, careful consideration must be given to the criteria for awarding the scholarship. Institutions that have established such scholarships, including Virginia Tech, Syracuse University, and Texas A&M University, have chosen to recognize those lost with a scholarship dedicated collectively to the victims. During the development of the scholarship process, it is imperative to include the families of those lost. Other institutions use scholarship criteria symbolic of the character traits of those students who were lost. At Virginia Tech, the Hokie Spirit Memorial Fund raised more than $8.5 million from over 21,000 groups, companies, and individuals in its first 2 years of existence (Virginia Tech, 2009).

From Grieving to Healing

In the days, weeks, and months following a tragedy, the community moves from grieving to healing. As the university plans activities and events after the tragedy, it is important for each event to build upon the previous one. Memorials, vigils, and other events planned by the university should be designed to help the community come together collectively and begin moving forward on the continuum from grieving to healing. The tone of each event provided by the campus should validate the initial shock, disbelief, and grief while still affirming that the environment is safe. As time passes, the message becomes one of resilience, healing, and hope. While it is necessary to recognize that individuals will be at different stages of the grieving process or will be affected differently by the tragedy, the campus events need to inspire self-confidence and community confidence and instill the knowledge that the campus community will prevail and recover. Additionally, it is important that the message of each event be sensitive in design to allow individuals to be where they are on the grieving continuum and to make progress toward healing at their own pace.

The language used is also important. Conscious decisions should be made about the message that will be sent in the name of each event as well as the choice of words in any prepared comments. A memorial sends a different message than a tribute or remembrance. Multifaith differs in meaning from ecumenical, and the 1-year milestone following the tragedy can be noted as an anniversary or a commemoration.

It is also essential that event planners anticipate who their audience will be. Not only is it important to tailor any remarks to those in attendance, but it is also imperative to think broadly about who is in the audience and to consider the needs of the community. Many questions must be answered including, should organizers provide a police presence so that people feel safe; are local, state, or national dignitaries planning to attend, and what are their security needs; where are the available event venues in proximity to the tragedy; and who are the most appropriate speakers?

When anticipating who the audience will be, special considerations are critical when victims of the shooting or families of the deceased are present. Planning an opportunity for families of the deceased to meet survivors and their families in a private reception or event allows the planners to create a more comfortable environment. The planning process also allows organizers to discuss and decide on small but important details. For example, name tags can discreetly and tactfully identify the family members of those injured and those who lost their lives, avoiding the awkward question of "How is your son?" asked of a father who has just lost his child. Blank pieces of paper and pens should also be available so that families can exchange contact information.

In planning public events where victims' families and survivors are present, attention must be paid to details such as shielding victims and the families of the deceased from the media by providing transportation from off-site locations, providing a choice of public or private seating at the event, and making provisions for the victims and families to interact with appropriate dignitaries. By providing special accommodations for these important guests, the university displays an exceptional attribute of caring.

Another crucial consideration in working with the families of the deceased or those injured is to determine what information they are

willing to have shared publicly. Because these events may be tele-
vised, and in many cases streamed over the Internet worldwide, it is
respectful to ensure that families are comfortable with any personal
information about the victims that is shared by the university. Any
photographs of the victims used publicly should also be approved. Of
utmost importance is that the university determine, with all certainty,
the most appropriate name to use publicly, understanding that institutional records do not always reflect the name associated with the
victim. Using nicknames may appear to give the speaker a more personal connection to the loss, but the name might not be recognized.
Additionally, the exact and appropriate pronunciation of all names
must be verified. It is critical that campus leadership, dignitaries,
and speakers, as well as the media, be briefed on this small but very
important detail.

Another issue for serious consideration is how to portray the perpetrator of the violence. Many times the ones responsible take their
own life. Institutions need to make conscious decisions whether the
perpetrator should also be considered a victim, and whether his or
her name should be stated alongside those of the people whose lives
were taken. As any institution begins its public healing process, this
is a sensitive topic that campuses will need to address quickly. This
decision cannot be taken lightly, as it can potentially divide community support and alienate survivors and the families of the deceased.
The community itself will wrestle with this decision, as demonstrated
at Virginia Tech and Northern Illinois University where markers with
the shooters' names—a stone at Virginia Tech and a cross at Northern Illinois University—continued to appear, disappear, and reappear
at the central memorial sites.

Religion Debate

During a crisis, many individuals turn to their faith for strength and
comfort. Many want and expect the institution to use religious references, symbolism, and prayers in the healing process. The line
between church and state becomes difficult to determine under the
stress of a crisis. Caution and intentionality should be exercised

regarding if, when, and how religious references are made. Institutions must make a choice about whether to use religious symbols, and if so, from which faith communities. It is also important to note that those who do not have religious affiliations or who feel alienated by certain faith traditions may be offended by the use of particular symbols and references. According to Eyre (2006), "Conflicts focusing on the organization, content, and symbolism associated with post-tragedy rituals and commemoration" (p. 448) may arise in communities with religious diversity. Leaders in the faith communities associated with the institution can be instrumental in providing insights during this decision-making process as well as assisting with the appropriate use of symbols and language during public forums.

As counterintuitive as it may seem, matters of importance are not always tied to the crisis itself when the focus is on the detailed planning and management of the public image of the institution. As Eyre (2006) stated, "Emergency managers . . . often find themselves involved in organizing the itinerary, security and media management of such [dignitary] visitations. . . . There can be a feeling that such time and energies might be better used in dealing with the more important tasks" (p. 445).

The involvement of dignitaries is yet another issue requiring sensitivity. When tragedy occurs, local, state, and national dignitaries may come to the campus in a show of support. In addition to the management of media and security, the institution needs to make choices about the dignitaries' time on campus. Many questions need to be asked: Who is most appropriate to meet with the dignitaries? Should the dignitary have private time with the families of the victims or the injured? Should dignitaries be part of a formal campus event such as a vigil or memorial service? Will media have access to their time on campus? Is the dignitary, or the timing of the visit, controversial or unpopular, and what are the implications?

The Message

A common thread running throughout all of these issues of sensitivity is the media. Without a moment's notice, the institution is catapulted onto the world stage. Each public event and healing initiative needs to be planned with conscious thought about how it will be portrayed on the nightly news. A number of important details that must be attended to by event planners include deciding on platforms, stages, venues, and lighting, all of which must be chosen and prepared with the television or camera lens in mind. Are all images provided to the media complimentary to the institution? Have all speakers been fully prepared with written comments that consistently communicate the institution's message? Any prepared comments should be carefully edited to ensure that common, yet insensitive, phrases, such as "We'd kill to have those students back with us," are eliminated. Additionally, comments should not include any descriptions or images that could retraumatize event participants. When the media are allowed entrance to an event, a designated area should be provided for them. This contains their impact but ensures that they have close camera shots of the event, clear audio, and are able to capture and communicate the moment so that it clearly reflects the spirit of the event. No event, regardless of the best efforts, can be fully secured from the media's presence, and attention to detail will guarantee a positive public image.

After the days turn into weeks, there will come a time when university officials must make a decision about the removal, archiving, and potential disposal of the expressions of grief, condolences, and temporary memorial sites. The administrators will need to decide when to remove the items, who will remove the items, and how the items will be preserved. Creating a policy regarding the management of artifacts may be necessary, noting particularly what items will be preserved, what items will be disposed of, and how the disposal will occur. Institutions can call on the talents of their community members, archivists, and historians, among others, to lend their expertise to this challenging task.

In addition to the preservation of artifacts, it is important to have photographic and video records of this significant though painful event in the institution's history. Institutions should be intentional about creating their own visual record. If this task cannot be handled by university staff, outsourcing this responsibility to a private vendor or public relations staff from another college or university may be necessary. Most importantly, those recording these historic events must understand the institution's archival needs in the immediate period and for the future.

Finally, the university must be cognizant of the fact that large-scale tragedies do not affect only the campus; they also have an impact on the surrounding city and town. It is important to remember that many of the first responders and hospital staff who worked to save the lives of the shooting victims are part of the greater community beyond the bounds of the university, and that they too need to participate in the healing process. Institutions should make a point of reaching out to the surrounding area and inviting the greater community to be a part of the healing.

Long-Term Community Healing Initiative

According to Jablonski, McClellan, and Zdziarski (2008), "One of the most difficult parts of moving forward is to figure out how to balance remembering with living the daily life of a college campus filled with the opportunity for learning, fun, celebration, and sports" (p. 30). Traumatic events are experienced differently by each individual. Each person is influenced by a number of factors including his or her proximity to the event, the intensity and scope of the event, the duration and reoccurrence of trauma, his or her appraisal of the negative stress associated with the event, and his or her emotional response to the traumatic stress (Herman, 1992; Klingman & Cohen, 2004). Research indicates that those involved will recover at their own pace and in their own way (Jablonski et al., 2008; Landau, Mittal, & Wieling, 2008).

As the institution makes a number of important long-term decisions, a gentle balance needs to be struck between remembering and moving forward. Additionally, it is important for constituents to feel they have a voice in the decision-making process. Research indicates that institutions must involve all community constituents in their recovery plan: students, faculty, staff, parents, alumni, community members, and others (Landau et al., 2008). Ensuring that the families of the deceased and those students directly affected by the tragedy have a voice in significant decisions is important in strengthening their sense of connectedness to the community. Decisions need to be made on opening and/or using the building where the tragedy occurred, the location and type of permanent memorial, and the use of money donated.

Eyre (2006) stated, "The importance of remembering the past is illustrated in the erection and maintenance of permanent reminders of tragic events" (p. 452). The creation of a memorial site, as with all other long-term healing initiatives, has "the potential for disagreement in the design, cost and location" because of its "huge symbolic and political significance" (Eyre, p. 453). The community and key stakeholders will expect to be asked to offer their input on this important initiative. If an institution chooses to build a permanent memorial, it is important for the university to provide an interim space for remembrance as plans and construction for a permanent memorial are formulated. A provisional memorial space should be designed and made available to the public. This area can include blank journals for visitors to record messages, a display of gifts and condolences sent to the institution, photographs and memorabilia from the memorial events, as well as a commemoration of the lives lost.

Making intentional efforts to create, or reinvigorate, a campus culture in the aftermath of a tragedy can bring a renewed sense of purpose to the community. As Zinner, Williams, & Ellis (1999) wrote, "The grief a community experiences after a traumatic event may become either a developmental crisis or opportunity for that community" (p. 28). The year following the tragedy at Northern Illinois University, officials used Boyer's (1990) Principles of Community to reestablish the campus community. These values were incorporated into the Northern Pact, an agreement signed by the university's students in which they made a commitment to create a community that is open, disciplined, just, celebrative, and, most important, caring.

Providing immediate, intermediate, and long-term healing initiatives should be an intentional, well-thought-out response to crises in a community. Just as campuses have reviewed their emergency preparedness plans, they should also develop plans for healing initiatives in the days, weeks, and months following tragic events.

Offices for Ongoing Support

One of the most significant institutional responses to address the ongoing needs that stem from campus tragedies is the creation of offices with the sole purpose of providing direct support to primary and secondary victims, and to the families of the deceased victims. Originating at Texas A&M University, and replicated by Virginia Tech and Northern Illinois University, a centralized office of victim support services was provided by the institution. The purpose of these offices, though specific in nature, is broad in scope.

These offices of support and advocacy serve as a vital communication link between the institution, the injured, and the families of those lost. They keep victims and families informed of university events and publications related to the tragedy, and provide important academic deadlines and policy information. They also provide the injured and families of the deceased with a place to voice their concerns and receive answers to their many questions without having to navigate a complicated university structure. They keep families apprised of forthcoming media segments, articles, and books that mention the tragedy.

In addition to facilitating communication, these offices help the injured develop social support networks. There is growing evidence of the value of leisure activities in overcoming traumatic events (Arai, Griffin, Miatello, & Greig, 2008; Hutchinson, Bland, & Kleiber, 2008). Despite their common circumstance, survivors may not know one another. Support offices facilitate important connections among students who have this unique shared experience. Just as critical as offering direct and indirect counseling, social programming provides the opportunity for victims to remember, reflect, and provide support to each other.

Attending not only to the emotional health of students but also to their academic success is a key function of these offices. It is critical for support offices to work with advising units and faculty to provide academic resources and guidance. Witnesses and injured students have a unique set of academic needs that range from informing faculty of the student's status as a witness of the shooting to rearranging course schedules so that these students are not in an environment that might retraumatize them (i.e., classrooms that resemble or are near the location of the shooting). The office staff also monitor students' academic progress when requested, and they discuss with students strategies to acquire special accommodations when needed. Faculty must be informed regarding potential sources of agitation for those who survived the shooting. Examples of emotional triggers include students entering classrooms after the lecture begins, just as the shooter might have entered the classroom, or the silence in the classroom during an exam that mimics the silence after the gunfire ended. Yet another example of the academic impact is the student who is hesitant to continue as an education major because a career in the classroom seems unfathomable after what he or she experienced in that setting.

Supporting the families of those lost and those directly affected by the shooting is an important responsibility of the support offices. These offices provide support groups for family members as well as resources and literature that can help families to process grief. The offices also equip families with valuable information, such as educating them about common prompts or cues that can trigger traumatic reactions in students. Most families would not know that fireworks on the Fourth of July or the sound of books being dropped can cause students temporary distress, as these sounds remind them of gunshots. The information provided by the offices is invaluable in managing the day-to-day stresses of supporting a loved one who has experienced the trauma of a shooting.

Support offices also serve the university by planning commemorative events, providing feedback to institutional leadership regarding the needs of victims, and serving as a voice for the victims and their families on relevant committees and planning groups. These offices also manage unique requests related to the tragedy, such as inquires about planting a tree on the campus in memory of a victim. Finally, these offices attend to the ongoing task of collecting and preserving the expressions of support and donations that continue to be sent to the university.

As the injured and those directly affected by the shooting move beyond the university, the mission of the support office can be shifted to serve the institution in a related but different function. At Texas A&M University, the support office still operates as a one-stop shop for any student who needs answers to questions or referrals to campus resources. Some institutions, understanding the value of an office that advocates for students with unique needs, have created offices similar in nature to the ones established to serve the needs of students involved in a campus tragedy. These offices are positioned not only to provide assistance to students but also to attend to any immediate short-term need that arises in the community.

Conclusion

An institution may respond to the task of healing a community following a crisis in a number of ways; providing safe spaces for reflection and mourning, moments of silence, candlelight vigils, and permanent memorials are just a few examples. While insufficient research does not provide guidance on what specific initiatives are most effective in the healing process, there is no question that when a crisis occurs on a college campus, an appropriate response implemented by the institution is expected.

The institution has a responsibility to provide opportunities for people to heal following a tragedy. These opportunities are the foundation for an institution to lead its community to a new normal. A university creates partnerships with a grieving, helpful community. Hand in hand, they move through the recovery process while challenged by many unfamiliar tasks, such as receiving the overwhelming number of expressions of condolences and planning commemoration ceremonies the world will watch. Throughout every component of the healing process, those charged with creating and implementing each event must remain aware of issues of sensitivity that may affect the grieving process, including issues of faith, politics, and integrity. A university should be mindful of its message to constituents, to the media, and to the world. Whether through programs, rituals, or policies, a university must also give consideration to long-term healing.

Most importantly, the healing initiatives in the aftermath of a crisis show the world the heart and soul of the institution. Although the community is faced with an inconceivable reality, "tragedy is the author of hope" (Bolman & Deal, 1995, p. 35). The response should embody the values of the institution and move the community toward a renewed sense of purpose and a commitment to move forward.

References

Arai, S., Griffin, J., Miatello, A., & Greig, C. (2008). Leisure and recreation involvement in the context of healing from trauma. *Therapeutic Recreation Journal, 42,* 37–56.

Bolman, L., & Deal, T. (1995). *Leading with soul: An uncommon journey of spirit.* San Francisco: Jossey-Bass.

Boyer, E. (1990). *Campus life: In search of community.* Princeton, NJ: The Carnegie Foundation for the Advancement of Teaching.

Eyre, A. (2006). Remembering: Community commemoration after disaster. In H. Rodriguez, E. Quarantelli, & R. Dynes (Eds.), *Handbook of disaster research.* New York: Springer.

Gersons, B., & Olff, M. (2005). Coping with the aftermath of trauma. *British Medical Journal, 330,* 1038–1039.

Herman, J. (1992). *Trauma and recovery: The aftermath of violence—from domestic abuse to political terror.* New York: Basic Books.

Hobfoll, S., Watson, P., Bell, C., Bryant, R., Brymer, M., Friedman, M. J., et al. (2007). Five essential elements of immediate and mid-term mass trauma intervention: Empirical evidence. *Psychiatry, 70,* 283–315.

Hutchinson, S., Bland, A., & Kleiber, D. (2008). Leisure and stress-coping: Implications for therapeutic recreation practice. *Therapeutic Recreation Journal, 42,* 9–34.

Jablonski, M., McClellan, G., & Zdziarski, E. (Eds.). (2008). *In search of safer communities: Emerging practices for student affairs in addressing campus violence.* Washington, DC: Student Affairs Administrators in Higher Education.

Klingman, A., & Cohen, E. (2004). *School-based multisystemic intervention for mass trauma.* New York: Kluwer Academic.

Landau, J., Mittal, M., & Wieling, E. (2008). Linking human systems: Strengthening individuals, families, and communities in the wake of mass trauma. *Journal of Marital and Family Therapy, 34,* 193–209.

Sandeen, A. (2006). Voice of the vice president. In K. Harper, B. Paterson, & E. Zdziarski (Eds.), *Crisis management: Responding from the heart* (pp. 64–67). Washington, DC: National Association of Student Personnel Administrators.

Virginia Tech. (2009). *We remember.* Retrieved from http://www.vt.edu/fund/index .html

Whitmarsch, G. (1999). Thousands mourn fallen Aggies. *Bryan-College Station Eagle.* Retrieved from http://209.189.226.235/bonfire/storyarchive/november1999/261199a.htm

Zinner, E., Williams, M., & Ellis, R. (1999). The connection between grief and trauma: An overview. In E. Zinner & M. Williams (Eds.), *When a community weeps: Case studies in group survivorship* (pp. 23–28). Philadelphia: Brunner/Mazel.

7 The Provost's Perspective

Campus-Wide Needs and Responses

Raymond W. Alden III and Harold Kafer

THE TRAGEDIES that precipitated the need for this book are never far from our memories. Personally, our involvement in providing comfort, guidance, and support to students, families, and colleagues has touched our lives indelibly. Professionally, as leaders with executive-level responsibilities, our skill at wise decision making has been challenged and is forever changed by the role we played in responding to campus tragedies.

The role of the provost at each institution is shaped by its history, mission, and the evolution of administrative structures in response to the needs of the campus. A provost is usually a member of the institution's executive team that might include the president or chancellor, a chief financial officer, and selected other senior vice presidents. Traditionally, the provost is the chief academic officer responsible for overseeing the development and success of all dimensions of the academic enterprise of the institution. Teaching, learning, research, service, and the infrastructure necessary to achieve these goals are the purview of the provost. Academic priorities such as curriculum and degrees offered, faculty affairs, student recruitment, enrollment, proffering of degrees, academic space, research capabilities, and the infrastructure required to support all these ventures are the responsibilities associated with the role of a provost. At many institutions, student affairs, athletics, information technology, and institutional advancement efforts may also report to the provost. The provost may also be required to have a professional academic background as a faculty member with tenure and a demonstrated research agenda.

Having defined the role of the provost and in preparation for the sections of this chapter that follow, it is useful at this point to explore the major constituent groups the provost will interact with during a crisis. The following provides a brief perspective from the standpoint of needs—what a given group needs from the provost and, where applicable, what the provost might need from these groups in his or her role.

President and External Relations

In a shooting, such as at Virginia Tech and Northern Illinois University, the executive leadership of the institution is expected to serve as the central hub for decision making and will be thrust into an environment requiring the communication of accurate information to all stakeholders, especially the victims of the crime and their families, and the media. In this context, the president and the public relations officer or designee will likely be continually engaged with external communications. The president is expected to be highly visible in providing information, comfort, and inspiration to the university community, its extended family, and external constituencies. The president will rely heavily on the provost and other senior leaders for timely and accurate information and counsel to be the face and voice of the institution. Depending on the size and scope of the crisis, the provost may share this role with the president.

Students and Their Families

Depending upon the level of the effect of the crisis, students and their families will look to academic affairs, as well as student affairs, for answers to the personal impact and the disruption of the academic routine and its restoration. These requests may range from the serious to the simple and may come first to academic units and colleges or via the crisis hotline. Nonetheless, the provost will ultimately be responsible for addressing these needs either directly or indirectly.

Other Academic Leaders, Faculty, and Staff

Other academic leaders at the vice presidential level will look to the provost for coordination of their areas with academic affairs and vice versa. Academic deans will look to the provost for guidance on their role in response and recovery, and what leadership they are to provide to academic faculty and staff. Academic institutions are first and foremost communities, and many will want to help in a time of crisis. The provost will be a key player in channeling that energy to good effect.

The complexity of the task of response and recovery for institutional executive leaders cannot be underestimated. Shaped by the details associated with the crisis they are being asked to respond to, each leader will rely on organizational leaders for information and to help them think through the intended and unintended consequences of decisions made. In addition, communications from executive leaders will be shaped by the nature of the crisis and the needs of varying audiences. In the event of a campus shooting, communications might be shaped by the degree to which the institution and its leaders may face legal action. In addition, communications to internal and external constituents by executive leaders are challenged by the speed of communications over the Internet. These realities, in combination with the constituent needs assessment, serve as a framework for deploying appropriate personnel and resources.

Unique Organizational Qualities in Higher Education That Shape and Influence Emergency Planning and Response

Deeply entrenched values at the core of the academic enterprise shape how institutions conduct their affairs. Some of these values include the creation and discovery of knowledge, individual and institutional autonomy, freedom of inquiry and expression, a commitment to shared decision making, and a pledge to strike a balance between the sometimes competing interests of the individual and the common good.

One of the results of these core values is that most medium- to large-enrollment institutions support an organizational structure that combines any number of semiautonomous units with diffuse authority (academic and support) that empower unit leaders with substantial autonomy to make decisions that affect their areas. Deans, vice presidents, directors, and others have responsibilities that carry with them a high level of authority to manage the affairs of their areas in collaboration with, but autonomous from, other units in the institution.

In times of crisis, diffuse authority may prove to frustrate efficient and a straightforward institutional response. In particular, clarity about who is in charge is necessary when implementing a crisis response plan that requires quick action. Diffuse authority (as opposed to a command and control structure) results in an organization where emergency planning and response may not occur efficiently.

However, when properly prepared, diffuse authority can result in nimble responses to crisis. In a culture that supports autonomy and in which authority is diffuse, individuals will respond and make decisions that employ resources within their control and within their spheres of influence. In the immediate aftermath of a campus shooting, individuals should not wait to receive direction from executive leaders to respond to clear needs. An institution will be best positioned to respond to a crisis when it harnesses this asset within a non-diffuse-response context. From our experiences, we have learned that big picture decision making, organization, coordination, and communication provided by an emergency operations plan (EOP) and the emergency operations center (EOC) that implements it does aid in responding to emergencies while providing flexibility and expediency inherent with the diffuse authority of a complex university structure.

Divisions of student affairs, and the profession that has emerged in the provision of support and guidance for students, are a unique feature of American higher education. In a crisis, student affairs professionals are frequently among the first to respond. As a unit, student affairs divisions are often set up with emergency response procedures and protocols that connect with on- and off-campus law enforcement, mental health, and other emergency responders. As a result, professionals in student affairs are viewed as first responders with responsibilities to manage crises.

Decision Making in Real Time During Crises

People often ask the leadership at our institutions a difficult question: How do you plan for the sort of unimaginable, unthinkable, unspeakable tragedy that your campus has endured? The answer is that while nobody can plan for all contingencies in a crisis of the sort we have faced, campus administrators do need to imagine the worst-case scenarios, think about their responses, and talk about crisis/emergency management. Moreover, universities need to create a comprehensive EOP that is continually updated and refined, based on the experiences of others. Of course, belief in this approach is one of the reasons that we are sharing the experiences of our campuses. We must all learn from the experiences of each other and refine our emergency planning efforts.

Based on the experiences at Virginia Tech and Northern Illinois University, several key components of preparedness emerge as essential to enable the institution to respond effectively and make the best decisions it can.

Academic Impact and Accommodations

One of the challenging aspects of a campus shooting is the cancellation of classes and the academic chain of events that results from that decision. Any unplanned disruption of the academic calendar of more than a day or two necessitates the rescheduling of any number of institutional activities. Additionally, buildings may need to be taken out of use temporarily or permanently. This adds a second and equally complex set of challenges to the mix. The provost is ultimately responsible for coordinating the response to such disruption and will rely heavily on deans and department chairs for a curricular response, the chief student affairs officer for assistance with student issues beyond the classroom, and the chief facilities officer for facilities issues.

The timing of the incident in the academic year also will be a principal consideration of what actions will be taken. The incidents at Virginia Tech and Northern Illinois University provide clear examples on this point. Virginia Tech's shooting occurred late in the spring semester, and a decision was made to cancel the remainder of the semester. Northern Illinois University's shooting took place early in the spring semester, and a decision was made to resume classes after 1 week and to extend the semester by 1 week. Each of these decisions created its own chain of events with some similarities but with more differences.

The following is an attempt to summarize the areas any institution's leaders will need to be prepared in to act from the academic perspective in the face of a campus shooting.

Academic Calendar

Decisions will have to be made about cancellation and resumption of classes. Consideration will need to be given to the issue of course content and how or if courses will be completed. Circumstances may require the provost to amend the calendar for a semester or even an academic year. Next, a host of unintended consequences will need to be addressed. The institution will likely have to respond to questions on academic policy, such as potential waivers or temporary exceptions; flexibility regarding grading issues; scheduling of curricular activities such as field trips, clinicals, performances, and so forth; and disruptions of other kinds. At Northern Illinois University, for example, a large number of international students had purchased advanced airfare to their home countries prior to the decision to extend the semester and were faced with substantial financial loss if they were forced to reschedule. The university staff contacted all major airlines and asked to exchange those tickets for a later departure date.

Student Issues

Students may seek relief for a variety of issues following a shooting incident, as noted in chapters 3 and 4. Many may lose their focus and require extraordinary academic accommodations. Institutions should anticipate an increase in requests for medical withdrawals, incompletes, accommodations for exams, and other academic assistance. Depending on the number and nature of such requests, an institutional policy review may be necessary.

Special academic accommodations may be required for certain groups of students. The students identified as those most affected by the shootings at Northern Illinois University (i.e., the victims who were present at the time of the shootings) were each assigned counselors and academic advisers as liaisons. The academic advisers ensured that these students were tracked closely and were provided with any special academic accommodations that were needed.

Faculty Issues

Faculty members too may seek relief for a variety of issues. Faculty members, instructors, and graduate teaching assistants may need training on how to deal with students in their classes who are experiencing the various levels of stress associated with mass violence. During the week that the Northern Illinois University campus was closed following the shootings, over 80 workshops were held to provide faculty and staff with counseling support and training on how to support students returning to their classes. Counseling center directors from Virginia Tech, the University of Arkansas, and Northern Illinois University, as well as employee assistant program counselors, led workshops for faculty, graduate teaching assistants, and staff members from each academic department. Volunteer counselors were available in each classroom during the first day of classes to provide direct support for the faculty in dealing with their students (see chapter 4, p. 93). Counseling support services were made available to all faculty and staff who felt they needed additional one-on-one support during the months following the shootings.

Concerns about how faculty and staff should deal with disturbed students who may pose a threat to themselves or others may require additional training. At Northern Illinois University, training workshops on this topic are routinely offered. In addition, folders containing a convenient guide and decision tree about the policies, procedures, and resource contacts available to address this issue are distributed annually to all faculty and staff (see chapter 3, p. 69).

Probationary faculty may have concerns about their progress toward tenure for reasons such as an inability to focus and a fear that their teaching or research may suffer; their reliance on graduate assistants who may have been adversely affected by the incident; and other career interruptions. Again, policy issues and accommodations may come into play. Counseling and mentoring services should be made available to individuals who have stress-related or productivity issues following the crisis.

Facilities Issues

A shooting may result in short-term, intermediate, or even permanent closure of one or more buildings. Certainly a crime scene must be secured, but the issue of emotional/psychological comfort for anyone returning to the scene of a crime, especially for those who were most directly affected, must be addressed. Depending upon the nature of the facility or facilities and the length of closure, a large and complex set of challenges may emerge. This was the case at Northern Illinois University where Cole Hall remains closed. Because Cole Hall housed the two largest lecture halls on campus (over 12,000 students took classes in this facility each academic year), and because of the technology available in those halls, two problems had to be addressed. First, for the university to resume classes within a week, classes in Cole had to be reassigned to other spaces that could accommodate large lecture sessions and, to the degree possible, with similar technology available to support instruction. This necessitated displacing another set of classes, and so on, until the process finished. The successful rearrangement of classes necessitated quick access to information on classroom seating capacities and course enrollment figures. Success also required coordination between the provost's office, deans, department chairs, and data offices such as registration and records. In all, over 150 classes were relocated.

Campus officials should be prepared to begin an immediate process of technology upgrades to classrooms to accommodate potential course migration. The cost of the response in these areas is considerable. Institutions should be prepared for increased personnel costs; unforeseen reimbursement of expenses such as for travel, supplies, services, and facilities; and other related expenses. For example, one institution estimated that the cost of additional technology upgrades exceeded $1.6 million, and overall costs of the response and recovery efforts of a shooting have been estimated to exceed $14 million to date.

The Provost and Student Affairs in the Event of a Shooting

In the event of a mass shooting, a provost will look to the senior student affairs officer and his or her staff primarily for information and coordination. Since the people in both positions are assumed to be members of the EOC, sharing information and coordinating responses ensures that recovery proceeds as smoothly as possible. A mass shooting fractures a community in a unique way. The goal is to rebuild that community, and meeting that challenge will be specific to the event and the institution. Suffice it to say that communication and collaboration presents the best opportunity for success in meeting the challenge.

Formative Feedback, Reflections, and Unexpected Experiences

This chapter closes with some reflections and some unexpected experiences related to the provost's role in responding to the crises. Several areas of concern can serve as road signs for administrators of any institution that considers planning for the worst based on our experiences.

The EOP and the EOC

Universities should have comprehensive EOPs (see chapter 3) and well-identified and trained members of the EOC. In fact, section

485(j)(1) of the Higher Education Opportunities Act mandates new requirements for emergency response and evacuation procedures for institutions of higher education that should be addressed by the EOPs.

Because of unforeseen circumstances or operational demands, the various members of the EOC and their support teams should be cross-trained and capable of filling in seamlessly for colleagues on a 360-degree basis (i.e., a matrix management approach). Leaders may not be available during any given emergency situation, because of travel or other circumstances, so the second-in-command individuals may have to fill in at the EOC. Moreover, decision making, coordination, and communication activities of the EOC may consume so much of key university leaders' time that others may have to assume more of the leadership responsibilities in the tactical implementation of the response efforts. Differential operational demands of each unique crisis may also mean that cross-trained individuals may have to be tapped to provide supplementary support for some of the response activities.

Communication

The challenge of wisely navigating multidimensional contexts that are sensitive to the needs of diverse constituencies is a short- and long-term concern. Multiple communication channels are vertical and horizontal in nature. Immediate information is necessary to inform those affected by the tragedy, as well as the campus community as a whole. Information such as providing immediate updates on an unfolding crisis, spreading the word about building or campus closure, providing an all clear when crisis events are over, identifying where to go for services and information, and the next steps are as important as the details about the tragic events themselves.

Parallel communication strategies may need to be implemented. For example, the staff of offices of student affairs or international programs may need to make contact with students studying abroad to provide information about an evolving crisis. Staff may need to provide similar communications to faculty, staff, and students at satellite campuses. Student affairs officials may need to take the lead in working with student organizations and informal student groups in coordinating spontaneous campus expressions of remembrance and sharing grief.

The provost's office should take the lead in developing internal communications strategies for the faculty and staff in the colleges and departments, giving special attention to the departments that have faculty and students among the victims. Group meetings with faculty and staff should be scheduled with clinicians and university leaders to provide information and support prior to their return to the classroom or other academic duties (see chapter 4).

Decisions concerning the cancellation of classes, changes to the academic calendar, and relocation of classes scheduled in the facilities affected by the crisis fall upon the office of the provost. However, the information gathering process leading to these decisions and their subsequent implementation requires close communication and coordination between the offices of student affairs and academic affairs to assess the readiness of the campus for the resumption of classes and the continuation of the semester. The provost also would benefit from direct conversations with deans, faculty, student leaders, and others in making decisions about how the semester should proceed.

Managing the "media tsunami" is a short- and mid-term concern. Within hours of a shooting, campuses can become overwhelmed with media trucks and hundreds of reporters. The sheer demands of the large numbers of reporters may tax campus leaders, support services, and facilities: for example, coordinating schedules for news conferences and interview requests; providing food and shelter (particularly during inclement weather) for hundreds of individuals; and meeting the space and utility demands for media equipment and trucks with the associated logistical and traffic flow implications.

Adding a dimension of its own to the complexity of communications, the magnitude of the presence of the media may add a level of trauma to the experiences of those affected by the tragedy. University officials may need to develop strategies to protect victims, their families, and traumatized students wishing to return to classes without undue pressure from the news media. While some members of the media are respectful, others may be relentless in pursuit of a story, with little regard for those most affected by a tragedy. Reporters may try to gain access to information about a deceased victim by passing themselves off as a family member, clergy, or counselor. For campuses with significant populations of international students, attention may have to be paid to communications with families and, in some cases, foreign consulates that are seeking information on the status of the emergency or about the health and safety of individual students. These constituencies may not have ready access to the information flow through news media and may have language barriers or differences in cultural perspectives (particularly related to sensitivity to violence) that may limit the utility of hotline interactions. Experts from offices overseeing international programs or from foreign language departments may help to complement the hotlines in communicating with these populations.

Factual information conflated with speculation is a short- and long-term concern. Furthermore, communications may become increasingly complex as the needs of a variety of audiences diverge and conflict.

Volunteer Assistance

Members of the campus community may be called upon to perform duties beyond their area of expertise. In a crisis of magnitude that deeply affects numerous members of the university community, inviting the assistance of external agencies with experience and resources designed to be accessed in times of emergency will increase the effectiveness of the campus response. This assistance brings with it an additional set of logistical challenges an institution must respond to (see chapter 3).

Campus leaders and their extended crisis response teams may be so focused on response efforts that campus community members who are not formally involved in these efforts may feel left out and frustrated by not being able to help. Once the initial crisis has passed, members of the EOC should communicate with the leadership of campus groups, such as staff councils and student organizations, to facilitate coordination of these individuals in ancillary volunteer efforts (i.e., planning grief/comfort activities, making memorial ribbons, signs of support, and other memorabilia, etc.).

Communication and coordination with the local community should also receive attention. Institutions in crisis experience an outpouring of assistance from the local community from individuals and organizations, bringing the additional challenges of briefings and coordination.

Unsolicited monetary support also may be offered by a large number of individuals and organizations. Virginia Tech and Northern Illinois University found that the least complicated mechanism to handle these donations was to create a scholarship endowment to memorialize the group of students lost in the shootings. Expressions of gratitude and information updates of the status of the scholarship funds and the awards process required attention by campus leaders and staff.

Financial and Legal Issues

Response and recovery efforts are extremely expensive, and purchasing goods and services has to be done in real time. The primary concerns of securing the safety of the campus, supporting the victims and their families, and returning the campus to its educational mission are paramount. When it comes to the response and recovery effort, campus leaders need to make it happen and worry about the financial impact later. Purchasing policies may have to be waived and procedures expedited or short-circuited. State and federal grants are available to defray some of the costs, but the financial impact may last for many months.

Potential litigation and insurance issues also need to be addressed. Legal experts at the university must be involved with campus leadership to advise and work on these issues as they arise. Campus liability insurance carriers may want to send in experts to advise and aid the EOC campus leaders in communication and response strategies.

Conclusion

The victims of any crisis and their families, as well as the community at large, will grieve and heal at their own rate. Campus leaders should be prepared to remain engaged in an open-ended way as the process unfolds. Virginia Tech and Northern Illinois University established quasi-independent, professionally staffed offices designed to focus on the needs of the primary and secondary victims.

The question often asked of a campus dealing with crisis is: Has your campus returned to normal? Members of the university community may even ask: When are things going to go back to the way they were before the shootings? Despite planning and all best intents and actions, the campus will not be the same as it was before the crisis. The hope is to create a healthy, new sense of normality, but with remembrance of the experience and sensitivity to the needs of those who are slower in their recovery processes. Those in an institution that goes through a crisis can develop strength of character and a sense of unity that are much greater than they had before the event. The approach to a new normality can best be achieved with the proper crisis management planning, open communications, appropriate and flexible responses, calling upon internal and external resources, and sensitivity to issues to address that could never be planned on in advance.

Campus leaders need to learn from the experiences of others and ask for whatever advice and assistance may be needed as the preparation, response, and recovery processes unfold. Administrators of institutions that have faced these crisis situations are more than willing to share their experiences and express their deepest appreciation and debt to those who have helped them by paying it forward and supporting those institutions that may experience tragedies in the future.

8 Too Close to Home

The Reality of Campus Shootings

Brent G. Paterson

IN WRITING this chapter, I share a personal perspective on how campus violence and, specifically, the murders at Virginia Tech in April 2007 and at Northern Illinois University (NIU) in February 2008 have affected me as a student affairs administrator. When choosing a career in student affairs, I never imagined I would be responding to the death of students, waiting for a student's family to arrive to tell them that their son or daughter had died, waking up siblings to tell them that their brother or sister had died, or attending numerous funerals of students at institutions where I have worked. While most of these situations did not involve campus violence, they still involved the tragic loss of a student's life and the resulting impact on families, students, and the campus.

My path began when the vice president for student affairs at Texas A&M University asked me to chair a small task force to develop a formal process to respond to critical incidents involving students after the death of a student at an orientation camp. Before the finalization of what would become the Critical Incident Response Team (CIRT) at Texas A&M, a student was murdered in her bedroom at an off-campus duplex, and her roommate was kidnapped. The perpetrator was also a student. Initially I felt helpless, but that feeling quickly shifted to implementing plans that were still in draft stage for responding to a crisis.

In the following years, the CIRT responded to numerous vehicle accidents, apartment and residence hall fires, and even plane crashes. In November 1999 the CIRT met its greatest challenge when 11 students and 1 former student lost their lives and 28 students were injured. The 59-foot-tall bonfire Texas A&M students were constructing before the annual football game with the University of Texas collapsed, burying the students under a mountain of logs. The response required enormous coordination involving university, local, and state emergency response agencies as well as other community and university entities. Although it has been 10 years since the bonfire collapse, tears still come to my eyes when I recall the incident. They are tears of sorrow for the families of the students who died, the students who still suffer from injuries, and the families who continue to support them. But the tears also reflect the pride I feel for the way the Aggie community responded to this tragedy.

Early in my career, I met with a student who described in a counseling session how he planned to kill his former girlfriend. It was one of the most frightening experiences of my career, not because I felt personally threatened, but because I believed the student would act on his threat. Weeks later, the student barged into the ex-girlfriend's residence hall room and opened fire with a shotgun. Fortunately, the former girlfriend and her roommate wrestled the gun away from him before the shots hit anyone and held him until police arrived.

These experiences and others have formulated my personal response to tragedies on other campuses. In such situations, I immediately think of my student affairs colleagues and what they must be experiencing; I know senior student affairs administrators at Virginia Tech and NIU. I remember what it was like to deal with multiple deaths on a campus. I recall the endless row of satellite trucks and news helicopters constantly flying overhead. I remember the long days and nights spent responding to the incident and trying to meet the needs of grieving students and their families. Recovery takes a long time, and everyone who personally experiences tragedy will never forget what it was like.

I keep a copy of a *Roanoke Times* newspaper article titled "Time of Rebirth for Virginia Tech" (Esposito, 2007) on my desk. The article reminds me of the good those of us in student affairs do even in the most difficult circumstances, and how we find rewards in the simplest of things. Ed Spencer, associate vice president for student affairs at Virginia Tech in April 2007, was in West Ambler Johnston Hall within minutes of the shooting of two students there. The tragic scene suggested an isolated act of domestic violence. Then, Spencer overheard the call on a police officer's radio that there were additional shootings in Norris Hall.

Following a sleep-deprived week of comforting students and their families, responding to constant phone calls and numerous e-mails, staff meetings, and media interviews, Ed and his wife, also an administrator at Virginia Tech, traveled to Pennsylvania to attend the funeral of a relative (Esposito, 2007). Following the funeral,

> He drove south that Sunday alongside a stream of Hokie-emblazoned vehicles filled with students returning to Blacksburg for their first classes since the shooting. Some recognizing Spenser's "ESVT" [Ed Spencer Virginia Tech] license plate, honked, and waved as they drove by. He realized then that he was part of a larger homecoming involving thousands of Hokies. (Esposito)

Any student affairs officer who has experienced such tragedies knows the pride that Ed felt in being part of a community that cares for one another and steps forward to help others when tragedy strikes.

Reaction to the Virginia Tech Shootings

While news of the shootings at Virginia Tech quickly spread, I found that I was more troubled by the incident than most of the students, faculty, and administrators at Illinois State University (ISU) where I am now employed. Ninety-four percent of ISU students are from Illinois, many from the Chicago area (Planning and Institutional Research, 2008). Perhaps I should not have been surprised that the campus did not feel a connection with Virginia Tech. A check with the registrar, to see if there were any students currently enrolled who had transferred or graduated from Virginia Tech or were from the Blacksburg area, identified one ISU graduate student who had completed his bachelor's degree at Virginia Tech. This student was contacted and assistance was offered. Student Government and the University Program Board organized a vigil on the campus quad for the following Monday where student leaders and administrators spoke. They also created a banner for students to sign that would be sent to their student colleagues at Virginia Tech, and collected funds for the Hokie Spirit Memorial Fund. Generally, the feeling on campus was, "It's not going to happen here."

On April 18, two days after the Virginia Tech incident, an international student walked into an ISU campus office and asked about the constitutional rights of international students regarding gun ownership and how he could obtain a gun. As one might imagine, the staff members were alarmed by a student asking how he could obtain a gun. Concern grew when the student was identified by staff as being "on their radar." That is, the precursor to what eventually became the Student Behavioral Intervention Team (SBIT) had been monitoring this student's behavior and conducting interventions to address his behavioral concerns. The student had a history of confrontations with faculty and staff in several campus offices regarding his employment, grades on exams, status toward degree, and university policies. The Community Rights and Responsibilities Office (CR&R) had met with him and issued a behavioral contract. The student had responded to his meeting with CR&R by e-mailing the president and other administrators, complaining that he had been treated unfairly by various people at the university. The assistant to the president and I had met with the student a week earlier to clearly articulate the university's expectations for his behavior and the potential consequences. It will never be known for certain what prompted the student to ask this question. Was he afraid for his own safety? Did he have plans to act out against others? Was he just curious about U.S. laws concerning gun ownership?

While investigating the situation further, it was discovered that the student had requested a travel letter from the International Students Office for travel outside the United States. A small group of university officials met with an FBI agent assigned to the federal Joint Terrorism Task Force to discuss the growing concerns about this student. The agent listened to the university's concerns but indicated there was no current tie to terrorism and no criminal record that would cause the joint task force to act in this case.

Given the student's history of confrontations with faculty and staff and the student's question about how to obtain a gun, it was decided that the student should be removed from the university; however, officials were quite concerned that such an action might cause him to react violently. The university police contacted Immigration and Customs Enforcement (ICE), and the university requested that ICE deport the student immediately upon the student's dismissal from the university. After reviewing the situation, ICE agreed to begin deportation proceedings immediately upon his dismissal.

The dismissal and arrest by ICE agents was scheduled for Monday, April 23. The plan was to contact the student at his on-campus apartment, present him with a letter from the university notifying him of his dismissal, and have the ICE agents arrest him on the spot. When the agents arrived, the student was not at his apartment. Knowing a little about the student's pattern of behavior, the agents believed the student would attend the vigil for Virginia Tech victims on the quad that afternoon. However, the agents were concerned about arresting the student in the crowd. Since I had met with the student, I offered to approach him and ask him to come with me to discuss an issue. I would then walk the student to the ICE agents located just off the quad. As planned, a plainclothes officer and I met the student as he was walking toward the quad and escorted him to a predetermined location where the student was informed of his dismissal, and ICE agents made their arrest. The student initially was taken to ICE offices in Springfield, Illinois, and was later transferred to Chicago for a hearing before being sent to his home country.

The Asian community on campus was already concerned that it would become targets for hatred based on the Virginia Tech shooter's Korean heritage. Now one of their own, an Asian student, had been removed from the university, arrested by ICE agents, and was being deported. They thought there was a conspiracy against Asian students and feared for their personal safety. Not understanding the specifics, and with the university unable to share the details, some Asian students feared they would be sent home next. Staff members worked to assure the Asian student community that its members were safe and were not targets for removal from the university.

I spent the next several days responding to questions from students, faculty, and the media about why an Asian student had been removed from the university. In numerous telephone calls with representatives from the student's embassy we discussed concerns of discrimination and arrangements for uniting the student and his belongings, which were shipped to Thailand by the university. Reporters from Thai newspapers and friends of the student also called. In addition, people who had had interactions with the student and had been concerned about their personal safety contacted our office. These faculty, staff, and students were thankful for the university's quick action.

Within days of the Virginia Tech incident, the ISU president appointed a task force to review campus safety and security and make recommendations. As a result, models for threat assessment and behavioral intervention were explored. That summer, the SBIT was established "to indentify, monitor, and, when deemed necessary, recommend appropriate behavioral interventions for Illinois State University students who display unhealthy and/or dangerous patterns of behavior" (Illinois State University, 2007). The SBIT built upon an informal process in which the associate vice president for student affairs, the associate provost, the director of student counseling services, and the dean of students consulted on students of concern and considered appropriate responses.

> SBIT members are expected to share information, within limits under federal and state law, about students who display unhealthy and/or dangerous behavior. . . . The SBIT attempts to intervene and assist a student before a regular pattern of behavior develops and the level of concern about behaviors exhibited reaches crisis level.

Members of the SBIT at Illinois State University include the associate provost, dean of students, director of athletic academic advising, director of student counseling services, director of student health services, university police captain, assistant general counsel, and the associate vice president for student affairs. The team has regular meetings and shares information on students through a secure database. A separate team addresses behavioral concerns about faculty and staff.

A wallet-size information card was developed to assist faculty and staff in determining when to refer a student of concern to the SBIT. The card also contains information on when and how to refer a student to student counseling services and how the dean of students' office can be of assistance. The card, titled "Helping Students Get Help," is distributed annually to all university faculty and staff. There is also a Helping Students Get Help Web site.

Another result of the task force was obtaining a campus emergency notification system, and following extensive research, a vendor was identified. Months of planning were necessary to determine how campus technology would interact with the new system, to establish protocols for messages to be sent, and to develop a marketing plan. Unfortunately, some administrators and parents view a campus emergency notification system as a panacea that will keep the campus safe. In reality, it will not prevent a random act of violence, but it can be a useful communication tool to quickly disseminate accurate information to a wide audience.

Shootings at NIU

Within minutes of the shootings in DeKalb in February 2008, an ISU director called the vice president for student affairs office to inform the staff of a shooting at NIU. A staff member had received a text message from her worried daughter, a student at NIU. The daughter was fine and had not witnessed the shootings, but everyone on the NIU campus was concerned about his or her safety. Word about the shooting spread quickly at ISU. Many ISU students had friends and family at NIU and were receiving text messages from their friends about what was happening on the campus in DeKalb. A number of faculty and staff had sons and daughters enrolled at NIU. Almost everyone at ISU had some connection to someone at NIU. Throughout the day, students gathered around televisions in the student center and other campus locations to catch news updates and wait to hear about friends and family at NIU. Everyone was horrified at the tragic incident, saying that *it could have happened here at ISU!* At least for that one day, the students at ISU lost their sense of invincibility.

Staff in student affairs at ISU initiated preparations to assist students who had lost family and friends in the NIU incident. As the names of injured and deceased NIU students became available, staff searched to see if any ISU students with the same last name might be from the same hometown. While this method was not foolproof, it led to the identification of some ISU students related to injured and deceased NIU students. Staff and faculty were asked to monitor student behavior to identify distraught students and to connect those students with the student counseling service.

Student affairs staff members were also concerned that the gunman might have some connection with ISU. What if the gunman had been an ISU student and had a disciplinary record or a mental health record? What if the gunman had been removed from ISU for some reason? Later, as information was released that the gunman was a student at the University of Illinois, the question became, "What if he had stopped in Normal (ISU) on his way from Champaign/Urbana (University of Illinois) to DeKalb (NIU)?"

Some ISU students lost family members and friends in the shootings, while countless others felt a special tie to the university that is only a two-hour drive north. Student government organized banner signings; the distribution of red and black ribbons, NIU's school colors; and a memorial service to honor the deceased and injured. The student counseling service sent staff members to assist NIU when classes resumed. Everyone at ISU felt a special connection to the NIU family.

Graffiti Incidents Follow NIU Shootings

On February 27, less than 2 weeks after the NIU incident, the message "ISU IS THE NEXT NIU" was found on a toilet paper dispenser in a campus residence hall. ISU police were called, a report taken, and the graffiti removed. The horror of the shootings at NIU was fresh on people's minds, as was a raised awareness of anything out of the ordinary. Threats, even those that could not be attributed to an individual or group, needed to be taken seriously. In this case, the threat was vague, lacking when, where, or how: At this point, it was an isolated incident. Although the police launched an investigation, there was little hope of finding the writer of the message. The university president released a statement that explained what had been found and the actions taken—police investigation and increased police patrols in the residence hall where the graffiti was found (A. Bowman, personal communication, February 27, 2008).

Late on February 28, ISU police received numerous phone calls about flyers distributed on campus with a threat that ISU would be the next NIU. No flyers were ever found on campus with this statement. Shortly thereafter, the ISU police began receiving phone calls about text messages containing threats. The text message stated,

> O keep my school in your prayers aside from yesterdays night threat that was put on our school we recently just received a threat given unto Wright Hall saying: Tomorrow will be a day that even God won't forget. Please just be aware if you are on campus.

The ISU police were able to identify the student who sent the original text message. He claimed a friend who overheard resident assistants talking told him this (R. Swan, personal communication, February 29, 2008).

That same night, the ISU police received information from the Joliet (near Chicago) police department that a citizen in that city had received a text message that stated, "ISU is the next NIU. If you go to class be careful." Again, the ISU police were able to identify the individual who initiated the text message as an ISU student who overheard some students talking about a text message they had received containing a threat that February 29 would be a day to remember. The student was trying to alert her friends to what she perceived to be a threat to their safety and unknowingly sent the message to an unsuspecting citizen in Joliet (Swan, personal communication, February 29, 2008).

Also that same night, graffiti was found in a residence hall restroom, across campus from where the first graffiti was found, that stated, "Your [sic] Next." Still more graffiti was found in a residence hall restroom in another part of campus that stated, "ISU Next." Rumors of guns being found in a residence hall prompted a police investigation and phone calls to the ISU police. No guns were ever found. Residence hall staff received information that a resident had said to other residents, "I could have done better. . . . and I want to go up to Watterson Towers [campus residence hall] and pick people off." This also prompted a police investigation that determined that the student was just "mouthing off" (Swan, personal communication, February 29, 2008).

The next morning administrative offices were flooded with phone calls and e-mails from students and parents voicing their fears about attending classes, especially large lectures. One faculty member reported receiving 140 text messages from students telling him they were afraid to go to class on that Friday. The professor cancelled the class. Other faculty members began to ask about their safety and whether they should cancel classes. The ISU-Teach Listserv became a source for faculty expressing their fears about teaching class. The provost's office issued the following statement to faculty:

> University Police report there is no evidence to suggest that text mes-
> sages and rumors of graffiti pose a threat to campus security. Classes
> should be held as regularly scheduled. However, students who have
> left campus or have expressed a heightened sense of fear should not
> be penalized for missing class.

What began as a text message to a few friends had become a huge rumor mill that was out of control.

While ISU police and university administrators were convinced the original graffiti was an act to gain attention and subsequent acts were copycat incidents, it became readily apparent how difficult it is to dispel rumors. Parents and students accused the university of a cover-up. They demanded that classes be cancelled and the univer-sity be closed until everyone's safety could be guaranteed. The presi-dent's cabinet met to develop a strategy to respond to the public outcry, while others worked on crafting a message to the university community.

By 10 a.m. February 29 the president had issued the following message to the university community:

> Yesterday's news regarding the graffiti message in Whitten Hall has
> understandably sparked a great deal of concern throughout the Uni-
> versity community. Rumors are spreading throughout campus today
> regarding further instances of graffiti and other messages intended to
> make the University community fearful.

While there is no evidence to suggest that the graffiti or the resulting rumors pose a true risk to campus safety, an increased police presence will remain throughout campus. Understandably, many students
remain nervous. Students who wish to remain in their residence halls
and apartments will not be penalized for missing class. All faculty
members have been contacted with this information.

I urge students to keep in contact with their parents and to let them
know that they are allowed to miss class and make up any missed work
at a later time.

We also hope that people will not add to concerns by spreading
unsubstantiated rumors. Again, we have all of our resources in place to
insure a safe campus community (Bowman, personal communication,
February 29, 2008).

The student body president sent a message to all members of the
Student Government Association to dispel the rumors and to encourage students to report unusual behavior. The student newspaper distributed a special electronic edition that afternoon with additional
information about the rumors and actions of the ISU police and the
administration. These actions began to quell the fears of the university community.

Unfortunately, the acts of graffiti did not end on that Friday. On
Sunday graffiti was found in yet another residence hall restroom.
This time it read, "Death is only the beginning." On Monday, a sign
in a residence hall stairway was found altered. Someone had taken a
black marker and drawn a gun on the sign with the words "Oh cool,
guns." Monday afternoon, graffiti was discovered in a women's restroom in the student center. The message read, "You all thought/It
was a joke . . . /24 days left = Bang . . . Bang." That night a message
was found in a men's restroom in the library that read, "ISU is Next"
(Swan, personal communication, March 3, 2008).

The graffiti appeared to be acts of copycats, but fears remained
high. The university police continued to investigate each incident,
and the university took each incident seriously. Police patrols of the
campus, specifically residence halls, were increased. If there had
been any perception of an imminent threat to campus safety, action
would have been taken immediately, including notifying the university community.

On March 5 a message was found in the same restroom where the first graffiti was found 7 days earlier that read, "NIU 3/6 die" (Swan, personal communication, March 5, 2008). As with the other graffiti messages, there was concern that it could be real. Staff and students were on high alert. There was no activity beyond the graffiti messages to suggest something might happen. The numerous messages seemed to be the work of different individuals—handwriting, style, location, all were different. Spring break could not come soon enough!

Staff remained alert the rest of the semester. Although anticipated, there were no more acts of graffiti after spring break that referred to the NIU shootings.

Conclusion

Apparent random acts of violence are becoming commonplace in America. As reported on CNN (2009), "More Americans have been killed in mass shootings over the past month (March–April 2009) than have died in Iraq so far this year." This is a startling statement. Ironically, later on the day this news piece aired, two students died in an apparent murder-suicide at a Michigan community college, and a student killed himself after shooting three people at a college in Athens, Greece.

For at least the immediate future, colleges cannot let down their guard. Maintaining a safe and secure campus requires the cooperation and assistance of every member of the university campus; we must not become desensitized to this violence. A study by the U.S. Department of Education and the U.S. Secret Service found that "targeted violence is the end result of an understandable and often discernible process of thinking and behavior" (Fein et al., 2002, p. 30). Acts of violence are rarely spontaneous, but they are a dynamic process. Deisinger, Randazzo, O'Neil, and Savage (2008) describe this process in four steps that perpetrators often take in response to a real or perceived injustice:

1. Ideation to do harm
2. Plan to carry out the harm

3. Preparation to carry out the plan including obtaining weapons
4. Implementing the plan (p. 26).

Prevention requires an awareness of personal safety and a willingness to report suspicious behaviors. Prior to the shootings at Virginia Tech and NIU, the understanding among many faculty and staff regarding unusual behavior by students is represented in the following statement by a university counseling center director:

> Writing a scary story is not against the law. Odd behavior is not a crime. Not talking to people is not a crime. . . . You have to wait for someone to do something, and sometimes the first step can be murder. (Ashburn et al., 2007)

Waiting for someone to commit an act of violence is not acceptable today: Members of the campus community should be expected to report unusual behavior, and a campus threat assessment team should evaluate the potential for violence and intervene when appropriate to reduce the risk of violence. A threat assessment process goes beyond just preventing campus violence; it identifies students in need of help, whether because of alcohol/drugs, mental health, or threatening behavior, and it intervenes to help students, faculty, or staff get help.

References

Ashburn, E., Bartlett, T., Carlson, S., Fischman, J., Gravois, J., Hoover, E., & Lip, S. (2007, April 27). Sounding the alarm. *The Chronicle of Higher Education, 53*(34), A6.

Deisinger, G., Randazza, M., O'Neil, D., & Savage, J. (2008). *The handbook for campus threat assessment & management team.* Boston: Applied Risk Management.

Esposito, G. (2007, August 13). Time of rebirth at Virginia Tech: This year that's especially true for the university's VP for student affairs, Ed Spenser. *Roanoke Times.* Retrieved from http://www.roanoke.com/news/roanoke/wv/127803

Fein, R., Vossekuil, B., Pollack, W., Borum, R., Modzeleski, W., & Reddy, M. (2002). *Threat assessment in schools: A guide to managing threatening situations and to creating safe school climates.* Washington, DC: U.S. Department of Education and U.S. Secret Service.

Illinois State University. (2007). *Helping students get help*. Retrieved from http://www.studentaffairs.ilstu.edu/vice-president/division_resources/Helping_Students_Get_Help.shtml

Planning and Institutional Research. (2008, fall). *Illinois State University fact book*. Normal: Illinois State University.

9 Incorporating Words of Wisdom Into the Crisis Management Process

John R. Jones III, Karen J. Haley, and Brian O. Hemphill

VIOLENCE ON college and university campuses has been a serious concern of administrators, and it is considered one of the leading issues currently facing institutions of higher education (Dunkle, Silverstein, & Warner, 2008). Additionally, on average 16 shootings occur annually on the 4,000 U.S. college campuses (Virginia Tech Review Panel Report, 2007). Compounding the problem of shootings on U.S. college campuses is that since 2007 at least 10 occurrences resulted in fatalities of 1 to 32 students and/or faculty members, many with additional injuries (U.S. Department of Education, 2007). The message to higher education administrators is clear: It is not a matter of *if* it will happen again, but *when* and *where*. Not being prepared for a campus shooting is no longer an option.

However, knowing that a campus shooting will occur again is not as important as ensuring that the campus has the appropriate planning and preparation processes. The words of Johann Wolfgang von Goethe, "Knowing is not enough; we must apply. Willing is not enough; we must do," remind us that action should be taken before the results of a campus shooting affect another campus. Thus, at a minimum, each institution must have a prepared response to a fatal campus shooting or a campus crisis situation.

Recent campus crises have made it clear that university administrators will be judged by three things: what systems campus officials had put in place to manage the crisis, the immediate response from university officials during the crisis, and their follow-up after the crisis. It is imperative that college administrators be proactive in preventing violence and prepared to provide a comprehensive response to a crisis. This means taking progressive actions to mitigate situations that could escalate to significant campus disruptions, having an effective comprehensive campus response that uses resources to protect life and property in the event of a campus crisis, and providing timely assistance to the victims and their families. The preventive steps and advance preparation not only assist administrators in being better prepared to respond, but allow in-the-moment processing to diminish the second-guessing that accompanies a campus crisis. Although many campus crisis management experts, speakers, books, papers, and so on offer guidance for higher education administrators regarding the crisis management process, this chapter provides insightful counsel from those who have experienced and led during campus crises and is intended to enhance the crisis planning management process. The chapter contains eighteen words of wisdom statements that are organized into five sections: Prevention and Mitigation, Crisis Planning and Preparation (before the crisis), Immediate Response (first 24 hours), Response (first 7 days), and Campus Healing.

Prevention and Mitigation

Words of Wisdom No. 1: Timely and extensive early warning systems save lives. If a situation arises that affects the immediate safety of the campus community, use all means necessary to alert the entire campus. Every university should have a mass notification system to communicate the alert, and it is best not to rely solely on one method. Employing multiple mediums to communicate the alert maximizes the opportunity for the campus community to receive the message, especially if redundancies are built into the system. Example of communication alert systems are sirens with voice alerts, text messages, e-mails, telephones, media reports, department and building liaisons, electronic message boards at the entrances to key campus buildings, and audible alarms in classrooms. When a significant threat appears to be contained in one building or on a small part of campus, the alert still should be communicated to the entire campus.

Words of Wisdom No. 2: Information sharing, students' threat assessment, and early behavioral intervention are proactive ways of mitigating student violence. Threatening behavior on college campuses is a serious concern for administrators. If college campuses do not take steps to address situations in which students are exhibiting threatening behavior or dangerous patterns of behavior, according to research the behavior will likely escalate, resulting in acts of violence (Fein et al., 2002). College administrators should employ a formal process that assesses students' threatening behavior and centralize the process to mitigate student behavioral situations by monitoring students of concern, managing the flow of information, and intervening when necessary (Dunkle et al., 2008).

Campus officials must ensure that relevant information is shared in a timely manner with key individuals on campus when a student is deemed to be a threat to himself or herself or others. This is not a violation of the Family Educational Rights and Privacy Act (FERPA), although many mistakenly believe it is, and believing it can be a critical misstep at many institutions. To paraphrase FERPA, institutions of higher education may disclose information from an education record if knowledge of the information is necessary to protect the health or safety of the student or other individuals (2009). We must also instill this in our students. We should teach that codes of silence over issues of concern or a person's distress may lead to negative outcomes.

Crisis Planning and Preparation

Words of Wisdom No. 3: Create a comprehensive student affairs crisis response management plan. It is important to have a comprehensive crisis response management plan that responds to different types of crises and guides the operation of the crisis team in coordinating and deploying essential university resources. Additionally, the crisis response management plan should include protocols for dealing with student deaths, student psychological issues and needs, and campus violence. Regarding students with psychological issues and care needs, the plan should include an Involuntary University Withdrawal

Policy for Threats Related to Mental or Psychological Disorders that allows a senior student affairs officer, or an appropriate designee, to withdraw students from the institution who pose a direct threat to themselves or others. The plan should also include protocols for working with the media and a procedure for coordinating with external agencies.

Words of Wisdom No. 4: Intentional selection of a student affairs crisis response team leader is critical. The crisis response team should be led by the most capable senior member of your team, one level below the president's cabinet. For example, the associate or assistant vice president for student affairs or the dean of students should chair the crisis response team. When the vice president of student affairs inevitably reports to the emergency operations center, he or she will be too consumed by coordinating and communicating with other college officials to fully supervise and dispatch the crisis response team. However, it is imperative to have a preselected professional who is seasoned and empowered enough to make critical decisions autonomously in a crisis scenario to manage the response to the crisis effectively.

Words of Wisdom No. 5: Practice makes perfect is especially true for dealing with campus crisis situations. No student affairs crisis response plan is worth the paper it is printed on unless your student affairs crisis response team rehearses and is familiar with the response efforts. The crisis response team should conduct mock, large-scale emergency drills annually; this will allow the team to function in a learning environment before it is called upon in an actual campus-wide crisis. If the simulation exercise includes campus police officers, emergency responders, and other external agencies, consider increasing the number and scope of exercises per year. After conducting such exercises, it is vital that the team process afterward what went well and what could be improved. This type of meaningful reflection aids in ensuring that potential pitfalls in the plan are addressed well in advance of being applied in a real situation.

Words of Wisdom No. 6: Preestablished communication messages enhance efficiency in crisis response. In reviewing your campus crisis response plan to identify types of crises and the steps to address them, work with your public relations and public safety staffs to prepare preestablished messages in advance. This expedites the communication process of sharing specific university information. In a true crisis scenario, the few extra minutes it may take to draft such messages are best spent elsewhere. Furthermore, crafting message templates when not in a crisis mode may influence the language used and provide the opportunity to review the messages for potential misperception issues.

Words of Wisdom No. 7: Public relations plans and message controls are vital in crisis response. Having a preestablished public relations plan is critical in providing timely updates and minimizing distractions from the crisis response. Public relations protocols should be developed in advance and should include centralizing the flow of information, the staging of media equipment and members of the press, and a logistical plan for large-scale press conferences. Sadly enough, administrators must be very aware of the image and legal ramifications of *all* they do, and the press plays a significant role in defining those images.

Immediate Response (First 24 Hours)

Words of Wisdom No. 8: Response to a campus crisis is everyone's job. Although your institution should have a crisis response plan for student affairs and an emergency operations plan for the campus, it is imperative to understand that responding to a campus crisis is *everyone's* job. This is especially true when campus resources are used to protect life and property during and following a crisis. The response to a campus crisis begins at the top of the organization with comprehensive planning and direction, and it trickles into every nook and cranny of the institution. Every person has a role, everyone is critical. Additionally, staff should be prepared to be asked by college leadership to manage many tasks outside their daily work environment. This may include staff at all levels—custodial staff, athletic staff, and faculty from all disciplines—pitching in wherever they can.

Words of Wisdom No. 9: Reach out to those who have experienced the trenches. If one learns more from experience than from books

(Kolb, 1984), then those who actually experience a crisis situation have a different perspective and vantage point than those who only read about them. You must reach out early in the crisis to your colleagues who have gone through similar campus violence situations and use their experience to help guide your responses. One cannot stress enough how beneficial this will be to your campus. Furthermore, you may not need to look far beyond your campus to find assistance from those with experience. You may be able to seek assistance from colleagues at local and regional universities or from those at neighboring disaster relief organizations.

Words of Wisdom No. 10: Develop alternate means of communication. Although the traditional, primary means of voice communication (e.g., landline and cellular telephones) are effective ways to communicate internally when the systems' demands are low, they can prove unreliable when the demands increase significantly. Traditional communication systems become overloaded almost immediately. University administrators must have an alternate, internal communication system available that they can use at a moment's notice. An alternate system, such as hand-held radios or runners, is integral to allowing communication with your student affairs crisis response team and with other key college leaders when more traditional communication systems are inoperable. This internal emergency communication system should be carefully selected; it should use a range of technologies and redundant features, thus providing a secure network that cannot be compromised.

Words of Wisdom No. 11: Police officers' emergency medical technicians (EMTs) training saves lives. Having all university police officers certified as EMTs is tremendously beneficial. A combination of officers' experience and EMT training allows them to react without hesitation, saving lives by administering on-site emergency medical care. In an unsecure area where danger is imminent, the area is inaccessible to external emergency medical service providers. Police officers trained as EMTs are able to save students' lives because only they can access the incident area during an active crime scene and thus provide medical service to victims.

Words of Wisdom No. 12: Open communication to the students, families, and media demonstrates care. One of the best ways to allay the concerns and fears of students, family members, and media is to create a mechanism that allows them to obtain information and have their questions answered directly by staff. In addition to providing timely information and updates on your institution's Web site, you should establish a hotline or make phone lines available for a call center to respond to incoming calls. You should have 15–20 preselected phone lines available for the call center that can be activated and staffed within the first 45 minutes of the crisis. A preestablished phone number should also be reserved that automatically routes callers to the call center. Finally, create a list of 50–60 university personnel, or other campus volunteers, who can immediately assemble and staff the call center based on the demand. Ideally, you may want to include individuals with a background in counseling, given the type of questions that may need to be addressed. Finally, because official university information must be provided to this call center, create a process to track and share timely information with the staff that allows them to respond accurately and consistently to the callers.

Response (First 7 Days)

Words of Wisdom No. 13: Develop an interagency agreement with local and regional mental health providers. Experiencing a campus crisis creates a demand for counseling services that will exceed your campus's capacity. As an example, campus-based clinicians will be engaged with students at the scene, leaving potential voids in residence halls, adjoining classrooms or facilities, with student organizations or groups, at the student union, and so on. Therefore, you will need additional mental health clinicians to fill these voids. In preparing for a major campus crisis, your university should have a preestablished interagency agreement with mental health clinicians in the area or community. It may also be helpful to establish an alternative schedule of operations for the campus counseling center that allows 24-hour services for a period of time immediately following a crisis.

Words of Wisdom No. 14: Know and use campus resources. The composition of student populations on university campuses is richly diverse, including different ethnicities and languages. Campus crises that have an impact on students do not differentiate based on those differences; therefore, it is important to be able to communicate effectively with families, even when English is not their primary language. If you have a Latino/Latina student population, or other non-native English-speaking students, it is essential to have bi- and multilingual staff members who can interpret for families and who can address the media. Thus, a vital component of any student affairs crisis management plan must include the advance creation and ongoing maintenance of a list of the institution's bi- and multilingual employees with their contact information.

Words of Wisdom No. 15: Liaisons help humanize your campus's bureaucracy during the crisis response. In responding to a university crisis, injured students and affected families will have specific needs and desired expectations. To address those needs and expectations, identify staff members to serve as victim liaisons. The roles of the victim liaison are to serve as an agent of the university in providing comprehensive, individualized support to the injured students and families of the deceased and to assist the affected students in navigating institutional procedures. In short, primary and secondary victims need to feel they are important. Because the role of the liaison is challenging, only staff members with a great attention to detail and the skills needed to work in an emotionally challenging situation should be selected to serve in this capacity. Liaisons should be identified and trained prior to a crisis to better prepare them for their liaison role. The training should include but not be limited to narrowly defining expectations for victim liaisons, identifying information that the liaison can share with families, providing guidance from university legal counsel, and providing information on state and county victim resources.

Campus Healing

Words of Wisdom No. 16: Self-care during a crisis is more difficult but more vital. On an airplane, an oxygen mask descends in front of you. What do you do? As we all know, the first rule is to put on your own oxygen mask before you assist anyone else. Only when we first help ourselves can we effectively help others. Caring for yourself is one of the most important—and one of the most often forgotten—things you can do as a caregiver (Family Caregiver Alliance, 2009).

Student affairs professionals, with our many responsibilities and focus on responding to students' needs, often fail to provide adequate care for ourselves or staff. Self-care entails maintaining a healthy diet, exercising regularly, and creating opportunities to rejuvenate. Additionally, self-care produces a better quality of life today and into the future. Unfortunately, during times of significant work demands or crises, we often neglect ourselves, which results in physical, mental, emotional, and spiritual deficiencies. Operating at a subpar level renders us unable to provide optimal support to students or staff members when they need us most. To be at your best, especially during a crisis, taking care of yourself will allow you to assist others effectively. Take care of your staff as well by faithfully monitoring them and making sure they are practicing effective self-care.

Words of Wisdom No. 17: Adding more guns to college campuses is not the answer. As student affairs professionals, we must all become highly vigilant and intentional regarding the banning of guns on campus. Most campuses have a zero-tolerance policy for guns, and the foundation of that policy is that campus safety should be left to trained police officers, not students. According to a report from the U.S. Department of Justice (2009), homicides of teens and young adults are more likely to be committed with a gun than homicides of people of other ages, and in 2006 about 68% of all murders, 42% of all robberies, and 22% of all aggravated assaults that were reported to the police were committed with a firearm. If college campuses were saturated with more guns, it is reasonable to conclude that there would be a significant increase in Clery reported statistics. Arming students and faculty is not the answer; fighting violence with violence only begets more violence. The answer to gun violence is not more guns. Instead we must take back our campuses by bringing a level of consciousness to the pervasive impact of violence in today's society. We must create a peace paradigm on our campuses and develop peace-seeking values among our students.

Words of Wisdom No. 18: Enough is enough. As student affairs professionals, we must address the question: Why is violence happening on secondary and postsecondary campuses? This ongoing crisis and complex question provides an opportunity for us to lead our educational communities in taking a proactive stance. We must begin to develop proactive programs, services, and policies that ensure that our communities will not be paralyzed by the fear of violence, such as mass campus shootings, hate crimes, suicides, or assaults. The consequences of campus violence, direct and indirect, are detrimental to providing learning environments that allow individuals to pursue their aspirations. We challenge everyone to work toward making our campuses and schools safe environments that are conducive to scholarly pursuit and knowledge attainment.

Born from the vision of Zenobia Hikes, Enough is Enough is a critical collaboration designed to create a new paradigm for peace and safety on the nation's campuses—elementary through postsecondary—by addressing the societal violence that has contributed to unprecedented violence in some of the very places our students should feel most safe (see http://www.EnoughisEnoughcampaign.org). The Enough is Enough campaign, a special initiative led by the National Association of Student Affairs Professionals, is a national program that focuses on educational enterprises through collaborative efforts or creating critical relations that are designed to prevent violence from escalating into school tragedies. In the words of Zenobia Hikes (2008), none are immune to terror. Many college campuses across the country have joined the campaign and are proactively stemming the tide of violence. For more information regarding the Enough is Enough campaign, please visit http://www.EnoughisEnoughcampaign.org.

References

Dunkle, J. K., Silverstein, Z., & Warner, Z. (2008). Managing violent and other troubling students. *Journal of College and University Law*, 34(3), 585–633.

Family Caregiver Alliance. (2009). Retrieved from http://caregiver.org/caregiver/jsp/content_node.jsp?nodeid=847

Family Educational Rights and Privacy Act of 2009. 20 U.S.C. §1232g; 34 CFR Part 99. Retrieved from http://www.ed.gov/policy/gen/guid/fpco/ferpa/index.html

Fein, R. A., Vossekuil, B., Pollack, W. S., Borum, R., Modzeleski, W., & Reddy, M. (2002). *Threat assessment in schools: A guide to managing threatening situations and to creating safe school climates.* Washington, DC: U.S. Secret Service and U.S. Department of Education.

Hikes, Z. L. (2008, March). Closing keynote address presented at the annual conference of the National Association of Student Personnel Administrators, Boston, MA.

Kolb, D. (1984). *Experiential learning: Experience as the source of learning and development.* Englewood Cliffs, NJ: Prentice Hall.

U.S. Department of Education. (2007). *The campus security data analysis cutting tool.* Retrieved from http://www.ope.ed.gov/security/

U.S. Department of Justice. (2009). *Bureau of Justice statistics: Homicide trends in the U.S.* Retrieved from http://www.ojp.usdoj.gov/bjs/homicide/weapons.htm

Virginia Tech Review Panel Report. (2007). *A massive shooting at Virginia Tech.* Blacksburg, VA.

About the Contributors

Raymond W. Alden III is currently executive vice president and provost at Northern Illinois University. Previously he served as executive vice president and provost and dean of sciences at the University of Nevada Las Vegas. He also served as director of a large multidisciplinary environmental research and education program at Old Dominion University. He was a tenured professor of biology at each of these institutions. Alden has a BA/BS in biology from Stetson University, a PhD in zoology from the University of Florida, and was a postdoctoral fellow at the University of North Carolina, Chapel Hill. He has been inducted into four academic honor societies, received several commendations for excellence, served in leadership roles of national higher education organizations, was an editor of three professional publications, and has been a scientific advisor to numerous state and federal agencies, including serving as an expert witness for a U.S. congressional subcommittee. He has been a principal investigator on over $26 million of grants/contracts, authored over 200 reports and publications, and made over 100 presentations (most invited) at professional meetings, a number of which focused on critical issues in higher education.

Carolyn Bershad has been the associate director for clinical services at Northern Illinois University's Counseling and Student Development Center since August 2007. Previously she served as staff psychologist at the University of Illinois at Chicago for 6 years. She has also worked in various capacities in student and academic affairs at the University at Buffalo, Pennsylvania State University, the University of California/Riverside, and the University of Hawaii at Manoa. She has a doctorate in counseling psychology from Penn State, as well as master's degrees in Asian studies and cultural anthropology from the University of Hawaii. Bershad has been an active member of the American College Personnel Association (ACPA) since 1999, is a member of ACPA's Commission for Counseling and Psychological Services, and is currently serving a second term on the commission's directorate.

James E. Brunson III is assistant vice president for diversity and equity for student affairs and enrollment management at Northern Illinois University. He earned a BFA and MFA in fine arts at Northern Illinois University, and an MA and PhD in art history from the University of Chicago. His numerous publications and presentations focus not only on student affairs–related topics, but also on interdisciplinary themes that address race, ethnicity, class, gender, and sexual orientation. He is the author of *The Early Image of Black Baseball, 1870–1891: Race and Representation in the Popular Press* (Jefferson, NC: McFarland Press, 2009).

Angela Dreessen is director of student involvement and leadership development at Northern Illinois University (NIU) where she has been for 9 years; prior to becoming director, she worked in NIU housing and dining. She earned a BA in social sciences secondary education and an MS in educational administration and foundations at Illinois State University. Dreessen has also worked in the Chicago public schools system, Peoria School District 150, Heartland Community College in Bloomington, Illinois, and at Illinois State University.

Gwendolyn Jordan Dungy has been executive director of the National Association of Student Personnel Administrators (NASPA) since 1995. In her capacity as a national advocate for students and the primary spokesperson for student affairs administrators and practitioners, she draws on more than 30 years of experience in higher education. A licensed psychologist and a nationally certified professional counselor and career counselor, Dungy earned BS and MS degrees from Eastern Illinois University, an MA from Drew University in New Jersey, and a PhD from Washington University in St. Louis. Under her leadership and that of past-president Diana Doyle,

NASPA responded to the late Zenobia Hikes's call to address and stem the tide of societal violence before students arrive at our nation's schools and campuses by organizing the Enough is Enough campaign.

Richard J. Ferraro, assistant vice president at Virginia Tech, has oversight of the health and wellness areas in student affairs. He earned his BA in history and government at Cornell University, did additional studies at Johns Hopkins University, and received his MA and PhD in history at the University of Wisconsin-Madison. He was a Fulbright Scholar and a recipient of the Prix de Rome awarded by the American Academy. He previously worked in academic or student affairs administration at Emory University, the College of William and Mary, Columbia University, and Bucknell University.

Karen J. Haley is an assistant professor of adult and higher education at Northern Illinois University. She earned a BA in mathematics from Washington State University, an MEd in student personnel administration from Western Washington University, and an EdD in higher education administration from North Carolina State University. Haley has previously served at North Carolina State University, the University of North Carolina at Greensboro, Southern Methodist University, and Western Washington University.

Brian O. Hemphill is vice president for student affairs and enrollment management, and associate professor at Northern Illinois University. He earned a BA in organizational communications at St. Augustine's College, an MS in journalism and mass communications at Iowa State University, and a PhD in higher education administration from the University of Iowa. Hemphill previously worked at Iowa State University, Cornell College, and the University of North Carolina at Wilmington. He served with the late Zenobia Hikes as co-chair of the National Association of Student Personnel Administrator's Enough is Enough campaign to address and stem the tide of violence on college and university campuses.

Brandi Hephner LaBanc is the national coordinator for the Enough is Enough campaign, and associate vice president for student affairs at Northern Illinois University. As a member of her campus's crisis response team and a lead responder during the campus shooting in February 2008, she is motivated by her personal experience to raise awareness related to societal violence and the influence it may have on college campuses. A native of Lisbon, Ohio, Hephner LaBanc earned a BS degree in accounting at the University of Akron, an MEd in higher education administration and college student personnel at Kent State University, and is currently a doctoral candidate at Northern Illinois University.

Linda V. Herrmann is assistant vice president for student health and wellness in the Division of Student Affairs and Enrollment Management at Northern Illinois University. She earned a BS at Northern Illinois University and an MD at the University of Illinois College of Medicine. Herrmann previously worked at the University of Nebraska-Lincoln, the University of Illinois College of Medicine-Rockford, and the College of William and Mary.

Barbara J. Johnson is an associate professor and department chair of counseling, adult and higher education at Northern Illinois University. She earned a BS in accounting at Winston-Salem State University, an MBA with a marketing focus at Ohio State University, and a PhD in education and human development with a higher education emphasis from Vanderbilt University. Johnson has worked in academe for over 15 years as a faculty member and administrator. Previously she held faculty positions at the University of New Orleans, Jackson State University, and Volunteer State Community College. Her previous professional experience includes student affairs administration, community college and adult education, marketing research and consultation in higher education and corporate environments at Wake Forest University Medical School, Peabody College of Vanderbilt University, and CB&A Market Research Group. Currently Johnson is engaged in two research projects focused on the impact of Hurricane Katrina on faculty and student affairs professionals, and in preparing campuses for human and natural crises.

John R. Jones III is an associate vice president in the Division of Student Affairs and Enrollment Management at Northern Illinois

University (NIU). Prior to joining NIU, he served as assistant vice chancellor and associate dean of students in the Division of Student Life and Diversity at Indiana University-Purdue University Indianapolis. Jones, whose roots are in Chapel Hill, North Carolina, received a BS in applied mathematics from Appalachian State University. He attended the University of Iowa where he obtained master's and doctoral degrees in higher education administration. As a senior leader in his division, Jones has led efforts to increase partnerships in student learning, shared his knowledge of student development with the campus community, and coordinated responses to campus crises. His professional affiliations include the Association for Student Conduct Administration (ASCA), the National Association of Student Personnel Administrators, and the American College Personnel Association. He has served on the board of directors for the Madame Walker Urban Life Center in Indianapolis and the Center for Academic Integrity. He currently serves on the ASCA board of directors. He is a member of Omega Psi Phi.

Harold A. Kafer serves as deputy provost at Northern Illinois University (NIU) where he was director of the School of Music from 1991 to 1994 and dean of the College of Visual and Performing Arts from 1994 to 2008. He holds a BM in piano performance from the Peabody Conservatory of Music, an MM in piano performance from Arizona State University, and a PhD in college teaching/music from the University of North Texas. Kafer previously held faculty positions at several community colleges in Arizona and Texas, and was chair of the Department of Music at Auburn University for 7 years prior to joining NIU.

Courtney Knowles is executive director of the Jed Foundation, a national nonprofit working to reduce emotional distress and prevent suicide among college students. He has nearly 15 years' experience managing nonprofit organizations and leading social awareness campaigns for a diverse list of nonprofit and corporate clients, including Outward Bound, March of Dimes, General Electric, Anheuser-Busch, and the Equality in Marriage Institute. Under his direction, the Jed Foundation's programming and campaigns have expanded to over 1,500 campuses and earned a Peabody Award and two Emmy nominations. Knowles holds a BS in communications from Florida State University.

Thomas L. Krepel became president of Fairmont State University in West Virginia in June 2009. A lifelong educator, Krepel has extensive experience in postsecondary education and public policy processes. A native of Nebraska, he received his BS, MEd, and PhD degrees from the University of Nebraska-Lincoln (UNL). From 1986 to 1990 he worked in several capacities at UNL, including assistant to the chancellor and director of university relations, and was a member of the graduate faculty. He also served on the staff of the Nebraska legislature for several years while doing graduate work at UNL.

Krepel began his career in education as a junior high social studies teacher. He also has served as an assistant professor in the Department of Educational Leadership and Foundations at the University of New Orleans and was an associate professor and a member of the graduate faculty at St. Cloud State University in Minnesota. For 5 years, Krepel was dean of university outreach at Texas A&M University-Corpus Christi and a member of the graduate faculty in educational administration. He served for 1 year as senior vice president for academic and student affairs and 7 years as president at Chadron State College in Nebraska. Prior to joining Fairmont State University, he served for 4 years as assistant to the president at Northern Illinois University.

Krepel served over 15 years as a member of the volunteer emergency response service (i.e., fire, emergency medical) in Nebraska.

David A. LaBanc serves as director of residential operations for housing and dining at Northern Illinois University. He earned a BA in management, an MBA from Baldwin-Wallace College in Berea, Ohio, and an MEd from Kent State University. Prior to working at Northern Illinois University, and over the course of his 13 years in higher education, he has held either student affairs or development/alumni relations positions at the University of North Carolina-Wilmington, Baldwin-Wallace College, and Elmhurst College in Illinois. In addition to his campus duties, LaBanc is an active member of the International Executive Council of Pi Lambda Phi Fraternity.

Blanche McHugh is associate director for residential administration at Northern Illinois University (NIU). She earned a BA in sociology and an EdS in counselor education at the University of Florida. McHugh has been working in the university housing field for over 35 years. She coordinated NIU housing student security staff for 10 years and is an active member in campus and community interpersonal violence prevention and response efforts.

Brent G. Paterson serves as senior associate vice president for student affairs and clinical associate professor of educational administration and foundations at Illinois State University in Normal. As senior associate vice president, he supervises the Career Center, Disability Concerns, Health Promotions and Wellness, Recreation Services, Student Affairs Information Technology, Student Counseling Services, Student Health Services, and the University Police. He provides leadership for student affairs crisis response, and chairs the university threat assessment team. Previously, Paterson was a member of the student affairs staff at Texas A&M University for 17 years, serving in various roles including dean of student life. He is the author of several publications and was coeditor and contributing author of *Crisis Management: Responding from the Heart* (Washington, DC: National Association of Student Personnel Administrators, 2006). He is a recipient of the D. Parker Young Award from the Association for Student Judicial Affairs for outstanding scholarly and research contributions in the area of higher education law. He holds a BS degree from Lambuth University, an MS degree from the University of Memphis, and a PhD from the University of Denver.

Scott F. Peska is director of the Office of Support and Advocacy at Northern Illinois University. He earned his BS in broadcast journalism and his MS in communications at Illinois State University. He is currently working on an EdD in higher education administration at the University of Illinois at Urbana-Champaign. Previously, Peska worked at the University of Illinois-Urbana-Champaign and Illinois State University. He currently serves as the Region IV-East chair of the Campus Safety Knowledge Community of the National Association of Student Personnel Administrators and the Region IV-East coordinator of the Enough is Enough campaign to stem the tide of societal violence on college and university campuses.

Gregory Roberts is executive director and senior operating officer of the College Student Educators International headquartered in Washington, DC. He earned his BSc and MS degrees from Indiana University-Bloomington, an educational specialist degree from the University of Missouri-Kansas City, and a certificate in educational management from Harvard University's Graduate School of Education. Roberts is a member of Omicron Delta Kappa and Phi Delta Kappa. Previously, he worked as vice president for student affairs at the University of St. Thomas, a position he held for 11 years. He has served as president of the American College Personnel Association and the Missouri College Personnel Association. Mr. Roberts currently serves as a member of the Washington Higher Education Secretariat, the Council of Higher Education Management Associations, and is a founding member of the Higher Education Associations Sustainability Consortium. He is on the board of directors of the Washington Internship Institute, the Bacchus Network, and is an active member of the Rotary Club of Capitol Hill, serving as a member at large on its Executive Committee.

Micky M. Sharma is director of the Counseling and Student Development Center at Northern Illinois University. He specializes in the treatment of mental health issues of college and university students. Sharma's career includes service in six university counseling centers where he has worked as a clinician and an operations and training administrator. In addition, he has served as a board member for the Association of Counseling Center Training Agencies and currently serves in the council position for the Disaster Response Network for the Illinois Psychological Association. Sharma received his PsyD in clinical psychology from the Illinois School of Professional Psychology/Chicago Campus, and in 2008 received the Distinguished Alumni award from that institution.

Michael J. Stang is executive director of housing and dining at Northern Illinois University. He earned a BS in business administration at Drake University and an MA in higher education administration from Ohio State University. He previously worked at Marquette University in Milwaukee, Wisconsin.

Monica M. Treviño is vice president for enrollment management at the University of Science and Arts of Oklahoma in Chickasha. She earned a BA in English and a master's of public administration at the University of Texas-Pan American. Treviño has also worked at Northern Illinois University, Aurora University, and the University of Texas-Pan American.

Kelly S. Wesener is assistant vice president for student services at Northern Illinois University. She holds a doctorate in education from Indiana University with an emphasis in higher education administration, an MS in college student personnel from Western Illinois University, and a bachelor's degree in communications from the University of Wisconsin, Stevens Point. Wesener previously worked at Southeast Missouri State University, Hope College, Indiana University, and the University of Wisconsin, La Crosse.

Index